T0062322

100 Papers

a collection of prose poems
& flash fiction

Liesl Jobson

First published in 2008 by Botsotso Publishing
Box 30952 Braamfontein, 2017, South Africa
email: botsotso@artslink.co.za
website: www.botsotso.org.za

© in the text: Liesl Jobson
Cover photograph: Liesl Jobson

ISBN: 978-0-9814068-1-7

We thank the National Lottery Development Trust Fund
and the National Arts Council for their support:

A section of 100 Papers was approved for the degree Master of Arts (Writing)
from the University of the Witwatersrand, Johannesburg.

Cover & text design and production
Anna Varney
http://www.artslink.co.za/artstudio

To my mother, who taught me to read

and my father, who taught me to read music.

Contents

Shopping List

"Bread, oil, yoghurt, mieliemeel…" said Liesbet, clutching the phone on her shoulder as she unhooked the last roll of white loo paper from the spare bathroom. Back in the main en-suite she switched it with the empty spool. Would it last until she got to town to buy more herself?

"That all?" Roelof's voice echoed on the cell phone. She hesitated, fingering the last scrap of tissue stuck to the empty cardboard cylinder before tossing it into the bin covered in frilly yellow gingham like the toilet seat cover, tissue box holder and toilet roll cosy, now empty. These items of bathroom décor were gifts from her mother-in-law, hand-stitched and given them to Liesbet at her kitchen tea, with Roelof's sisters and aunts and cousins looking on like witnesses.

She would have to ask Roelof to get more loo paper. The last time they ran out because she hadn't written it on the shopping list, there was an all-night fight. Liesbet had wanted to buy it herself, because Roelof always bought pink to match the tiles and the towels, or yellow to match the crocheted toilet seat cover. His mother had taught him the importance of matching things. She said it showed a man's feminine side.

White tissue paper told an intimate story about Liesbet's private place, details she wasn't ready to share with Roelof. Not yet. Against the pink paper, she could not detect the faint spotting that heralded each failed pregnancy. Against the yellow, the subtle changes to her secretions that accompanied her fertile period were invisible; she couldn't see the discolouration that spoke of infection.

"We need soap, Handy-Andy and…"

"Hurry up," he crackled.

"Loo paper – please buy *white* loo paper."

The phone went dead. Had he heard? The reception at the farm was poor. She was two-and-a-half weeks overdue – eighteen days precisely. Was her nausea even real? Perhaps she was imagining it again. Her breasts were more sensitive than usual and her mouth tasted as if she'd been sucking a coin. She didn't want to go to the only doctor in Ulugwadule for a pregnancy test. The town was a railway siding and its name, translated from Zulu, meant 'the barren place'. In the bathroom she sat on the toilet. The cotton gusset of her panties was still clear.

An hour later Roelof's bakkie swerved up to the farmhouse and stopped in a cloud of dust. He burst through the swing door and dumped the shopping bags on the cracked kitchen table. He grabbed a beer and patted her bottom before slumping in front of the TV to watch the slaughter of the Boks by the All Blacks in Wellington. Liesbet unpacked the bread, oil, yoghurt, and toilet paper – yellow and pink.

In the spare bathroom she removed the hand towels with their beaming sun-faces embroidered in gold thread. She took the tissue box from its yellow gingham holder and peeled the elasticised toilet lid cover off the lid. Lastly she unhooked the lemon-coloured lace curtains and placed the whole lot in a garbage bag.

After stripping the pink bathroom the same way, she slipped out the kitchen door and made her way by the light of the thin new moon to the tool shed. She snapped open the catch of Roelof's blue tool box and unfolded each tiered partition, probing the metallic womb for a hammer, a mallet, a blunt-end chisel and a scraper.

The Organist

The Kleinfontein Christian Ladies Society committee members sat on the stoep of the pastorie and watched me collecting the stuff that called from the street. It was bottle tops that day, wanting to be looped together and made into a tambourine.

"That boy is peculiar," said the voorsitter sipping her tea.

"He has caramel fingers," said the dominee's wife, gathering her handbag closer to her with one hand and clutching the beads about her neck with the other. No one understood that it was things that stuck to me, not me to things.

"He will end up like Piet," said Ouma, wiggling her dentures. My uncle is an intellectual but a drunk, in prison now for stealing funny things from the apteek.

Last month, I developed a system for aerating the library fishpond, using the nozzles, tubes and pump bags I'd found in my uncle's cupboard. Correct aeration of a fishpond – preferably from the bottom – improves the water mixing, enhancing ichthyological resistance to infection. I read about it in *Better Pond Fish Health*.

At first, only the librarian was interested in the fine spray that spurted over the pond. I hadn't noticed she was there until her shimmering reflection caught my eye. Then the posmeester passed by, and he called the apteker over to look at my project. Next thing, Konstabel de Villiers arrived. He greeted us with a double hoot from his police van. He'd come to admire my handiwork too.

"Nice kit you got there, boykie," said the Konstabel. "Where did you find that bulb syringe?" I pointed in the direction of our house. "Very interesting," he said. "Do you want to show me the precise location?"

I didn't. But I took him to Oom Piet's cupboard anyway. The konstabel found his missing handcuffs in my uncle's cupboard. And some studded collars that had disappeared from the pet shop, too, but they weren't useful for my project.

The Christian Ladies' Society committee gossip when Ma is out of earshot. They think I'm deaf because I don't talk.

"Did she drop him on his head?" says one.

"He's a genius," says another.

"He's a tonteldoos," said Tannie Liza who found me reading *Die Ossewa* before I'd been to school.

"He's a liar," said the teacher because I blamed Chicken for the broken ornaments on her desk. Chicken, the redheaded rooster that perches in the peach tree, is my best friend.

I'd been teaching him to read from the Bible on the teacher's desk after the last bell of the day. Pik and Wimpie and Karel had promised to wring Chicken's neck and then mine. They would try sooner or later, so it seemed a good moment to convert Chicken.

We started with Luke, Chapter 22, verse 33. He was managing well with *And he said unto him, Lord, I am ready to go with thee, both into prison.* But when it came to, *and to death*, he skrikked. At *I tell thee, Peter, the cock shall not crow this day*, Chicken got into a flap. Down went the ceramic ballerina. Down went the porcelain shoe, and also the see-no-hear-no-speak-no-evil monkeys.

"That fowl's heading for the pot," warned my mother after visiting the headmaster's office. "You'd better learn to control him."

Two days later I sneaked an apple onto my teacher's desk. An apology. "You buying favour now?" asked the teacher. I nodded. She was still cross, even though Ma had replaced the ornaments. I didn't move even though I was dying to straighten the monkeys to line up with the shoe.

"What you want, boy?"

I wrote on my notebook: Chicken wants to play the organ.

"Go ask the dominee," said the teacher, rolling her eyes.

"It's just a whim," said the dominee's wife, who'd phoned my mother to tell her where I was. "It will pass."

"The organ or the rooster?" asked my mother.

"Maybe both?"

4

Now when we pass through the dorp, Chicken tucked under my arm, people stop and stare. I collect the key to the organ loft from the dominee's wife after school each day and we practise until dark. Chicken can play Bach's *Chorale Preludes*, Mendelssohn's *Sonata in F*, and the *Versets* by Thomas Tallis. His claws can't reach the pedal board, so my feet help him out with the bass. We did a concert on the radio. Every Tuesday when we cross the pastorie stoep the voorsitter of the Kleinfontein Christian Ladies' Society stops her meeting to say, "That chicken is peculiar."

Bump

"There's another baby coming," says my Mother.

"I have a bump too," I say. As I stuff a soccer ball under my dress, the seams split. My mother re-stitches the dress at the sewing machine that has an oily treadle that bites. When she rests, she lets me feel her bump kicking. We nap together on her double bed because I'm the big girl. Megan, the baby, sleeps in the cot painted with yellow chicks.

I dream I get stuck on the tracks at Sarnia Station, the tail of my bunny blanket catches in the rails. I can't escape the hissing engine, its blinding light and blasting horn.

Mother visits the doctor in town, and Ouma takes us to feed the pigeons. Bigger than Megan's head, the birds spiral around the statue of Queen Victoria outside the Durban City Hall, then swoop down in a flock to peck the peanuts Ouma scatters. I scream at them, but they keep following me.

Megan struggles to get out the pushchair with the fat white tyres. In the photo taken that day we wear matching striped dresses. My naked doll has floppy limbs; the stuffing pops out at the seams. Megan sticks a peanut up her nose. Or perhaps I do it to her. Mother goes back to the doctor with Megan. I want to go too. Ouma shows me how the frangipani trees bleed milk. Their poison will make you ill. The air is heavy with their sickly fragrance. I want to go home.

"Soon," says Ouma.

That night we eat candyfloss on the beach and later, as we walk back to the station, I pick up a wad of chewing gum that a man spits out on the pavement. It is faintly sweet. When my grandmother asks me what I am chewing, I swallow it and say, "Nothing."

We cross the road at the traffic light and I look back. Megan has been left behind on the traffic island and the cars roar past. Nobody has noticed. They walk on. I tug on my mother's daisy dress, trying to tell her that my sister has been left behind. I yank Mother's skirt, which splits.

"Now look what you've done," she cries. The men on the street spit; their spit keeps coming and coming.

How the Oreo Stole Christmas

Jansie plucked the low-fat frikkadels one by one from the pan. Moist shadows formed where they drained on the paper towel. She tapped loose the mincemeat crumbs sticking to each exterior and positioned the golden brown balls between pale yellow stuffed eggs, which she'd made with yoghurt instead of mayonnaise.

She dusted the display with bold chives and snappy paprika, placing a ring of cherry tomatoes about the rim, interspersed between juicy black olives. Against the cobalt blue platter, her dish was an artwork.

The unwritten rule of the unspoken contest defined the baking queen as the maker of the item that the minister sampled first. Jansie had privileged information. She had stood behind the minister in the Weight Watchers queue.

She paid no attention to Marta's golden koeksusters dripping with cinnamon syrup, even though Pastor Patrick had a soft spot for the sticky pastries. She did not feel threatened by Maryke's famous melktert, even though it had raised the highest bid at the charity fundraiser and nutmeg decorated the top in delicate and intricate star-shaped patterns. At the last meeting Jansie had congratulated the minister enthusiastically on being the biggest loser.

During the Nativity play the mothers whisked out their digital cameras, taking snaps of their tubby angels in silver foil wings and tinsel haloes. They tittered at the donkey that refused to wear its ears on stage, each secretly relieved it wasn't her child's recalcitrance provoking the communal mirth.

Jansie noted afterwards how the women studiously avoided each other's gaze when Pastor Patrick picked up a white china plate. She congratulated herself on her revised strategy. The weight loss counsellor had given a talk, entitled Surviving the Snack Table with Super Strategies. Pastor Patrick took a photocopy and folded it into his breast pocket. *Tip number one: seek high protein options to prevent a blood sugar crash.* That would be her frikkadels and eggs.

Tip number two: Find the fresh fruit and vegetables, but avoid the dips.
The cherry tomatoes. Even if the pastor helped himself to that first,
she'd still be the queen.

Jansie smirked when the minister passed over Maryke's melktert;
her heart sang as he waltzed past Marta's koeksusters, down to the
end of the table; and gasped as the pastor stretched past her cobalt
platter to snatch a little brown biscuit with a white icing centre,
imported from America.

The Science of Curves

I stare at the outline of Dr Henderson's bosom as she turns from the board, saying, "Introduction to Fractals is intended for students without especially strong mathematical preparation, or any particular interest in science."

Beneath the tight orange jersey, her breasts are snug, so much smaller than my own.

"Fractal geometry offers a new way of looking at the world."

By agreement, I don't question her in class. I do not need this credit; I want simply to observe my lover. I sit in front, noting how the cerise and aqua stripes on my socks swell and flatten as I flex my ankle.

"We are surrounded by natural patterns, usually unrecognised, unsuspected. Sensuous, irregular configurations occur in, and relate to the arts, the humanities, and the social sciences."

Her rounded buttocks sway as she walks to a window. Filtered light falls on her oval face. She throws the shutters open. Agitation flutters across her features.

"Examining the fractal curve, we see traces of complex dynamic systems self-organising into familiar natural shapes. Our understanding of the underlying mathematics enables us to model eroded coastlines, snowflakes, or the human vascular system, in which patterns recur on progressively smaller scales."

She ignores my gaze, hiding in her notes on the lectern instead.

"The determinism of chaos describes partly random phenomena such as crystal growth…"

Last night she wrestled her wedding bands off over her bent finger, her mouth a guilty twist. I imagine a supersaturated sucrose solution crystallising around her diamond.

"…fluid turbulence…"

Bath oil capsules dissolved in pink swirls, releasing the scent of vetiver and honey into the steam.

"…and galaxy formation."

I unclipped her suspenders, peeled off her stockings, sucked her toes, kissed the arch of foot. Her pelvis rocked in the water. Afterwards she said, "I saw the stars, the planets. They are so lovely."

Litter-Bugs

After Lerato's funeral, Grace saw the world from a peculiar angle. The doctor diagnosed labyrinthitis. If she tilted her ear 45 degrees to her shoulder, then the pews inside the chapel at Christ the King Elementary were nearly level and the stained glass windows rose almost perpendicular. But when she sat back from the kneeler after praying, the dark interior pitched about and she wanted to be sick.

She touched the walls as she walked along the corridors and held tightly to the banisters in the stairwell. When she looked down at the reading rug next to the puzzle rack, her eyes pooled and swam on the spot where she'd last held Lerato.

A week earlier Grace had written on the board: King's kids are not litter-bugs. The chalk squeaked and snapped in her hand. "Nobody gets lunch until that messy playground is tidy," she said. "It was in a terrible state after recess. Come back for your lunch boxes when you've picked up the rubbish." The bell rang and children raced barefoot past the chapel to pick chip packets and sweet papers off the grass.

Lerato clutched the curved garbage bin and flung a lollypop wrapper over the edge. She let out a small fluttery cry, jumping backwards on the grass, then ran, wheezing, to show her teacher the black stinger left in her palm. Grace was about to remove it with a deft scrape of her fingernail, when Lerato crumpled and fell to the ground.

"Thato, you must run for Sister Mary-Paul," Grace said to Lerato's twin brother who tagged along as she carried the limp child back to the classroom. "Run please, Thato," she urged, laying Lerato on the reading rug. The boy gasped in sympathy, staring at his sister's lips turning blue, as if he already knew that neither Sister Mary-Paul nor an ambulance could arrive in time.

The grade ones were returning for their lunch boxes.

"I picked up twenty papers, Ma'am," said Refilwe. "We got no litter-bugs anymore."

"Can we eat now?" asked James, shaking his sandwiches.

"Why's Lerato sleeping, Ma'am?" lisped Liza through the gap in her teeth.

"School is not for sleepyheads," said James, mimicking his teacher's inflection.

Jojo popped the straw into her juice carton and said to Thato, "Your Mama won't be pleased."

Interval

The harpist is a barren woman, fat and grey, and widely gossiped about. She sits on a swivel chair in the canteen, starting with a salad. They say she is always on diet. After she has wiped the dressing from her face, she tells me she is not satisfied. How can she play if she is hungry?

She returns with butternut soup and asks what I'm doing this week. I tell her I'm tweaking my reeds for the contrabassoon. The weather is changing, the rainy season has started. One day my reeds speak; the next they don't.

It is a long story, making contrabassoon reeds. She nods. I'm trying a new scrape on the tip. I want a sound that blends more politely. When she returns with a portion of roast chicken, she wants to know about my reed-making tools. By the time I am finished explaining the difference between a reamer and a mandrel, she is banging her fork on the plate. There are teardrops in her eyes.

While I draw a diagram on a napkin of how I wrap the binding, she fetches a portion of lemon meringue pie. Next she wants to know why my instrument always sounds like flatulence.

I return to the napkin, point to the diagram of the scrape, meaning to explain about the tips. I watch her eat, saying by accident, the challenge is to balance the lips.

A String of Wooden Fish

Two women on the restaurant balcony feed each other from the same plate. Paros Taverna in Melville has a Valentine's Day special: Eat all the oysters you can for sixty bucks. The blonde with the big silver watch and heavy necklace licks her fingers noisily. The brunette with bad skin blushes and giggles. It's easier to daydream about their sex life than to face Iris, my daughter who just flew from Cape Town for her first varsity vacation. At the airport last night I noticed how her head still looks too big, her skinny arms disproportionate. I said nothing, just smiled.

Iris picks the lettuce out her sandwich. Does that mean she will skip the sandwich and eat only the lettuce, or is it a less ruthless day, and she will eat the chicken on rye without the lettuce. She never did like lettuce. I'd hoped she'd try the meze. A rat scurries under the verandah across the street. I wish I hadn't seen it. The blonde takes the brunette's hand and sucks her fingers, closing her eyes, as if in prayer. I wish I hadn't seen that either.

The sun filters through the last feathery jacaranda fronds still on the tree, casting a dappled shade on our empty side plates. Spring is early this year. One tiny leaf lands in the sugar. I do not blink when Iris grasps a handful of paper serviettes. She started spitting out her food discreetly last July when her sweet little belly curved over her hipsters and a boy in her class called her podgy.

I stare at the fake mosaic on the wall, targeting something other than my daughter's plate. The image is a luscious nude carrying a round-bottomed urn. The psychologist at Tara Hospital said to back off; to allow Iris to regain control over her life, so she doesn't have to act out.

The picket fence surrounding the restaurant balcony is Aegean blue, matching the tablecloths, the colour of Iris's eyes. A string of wooden fish, hanging by twine through their gills, is the same brilliant shade. They remind me of children's toys. Iris reaches into her handbag for an envelope, unfolds a letter and reads aloud:

"Dear Ms Iris Sonnenburg, I am pleased to announce that your application . . ."

She never told me she was applying anywhere. The spanokopita goes dry in my mouth. Another course? Which university now? The sesame seeds are pebbles in my throat. What will it cost? Iris sneers at my alarm. I gulp my water. I don't know what she wants from me anymore. A flake from the bread's crust has fallen on the tablecloth. I try crumbling it onto my plate, but it is brittle, unyielding in my fingers.

". . . your application to work. . ."

A job? She never said she wanted to work. I've swallowed too fast. My chest burns. She'd always said she wanted to study medicine. With seven distinctions for her Matric and because she played principal violin in the Youth Ensemble, she was offered a music scholarship too. She accepted a place at the School of Medicine, but two months later she was hospitalised for force-feeding. The women on the balcony leave. The string of wooden fish remain silent.

". . . as a fish packer . . ."

Her tuition and residence fees. How will I pay off a year's fees if she drops out now? Perhaps if she gets sufficiently far away from me she will finally gain control over her life. If she faints and collapses into a freezer of freshly caught fish, might she find a lesbian lover to wrap her in kisses, make her round and happy again? Iris toys with the lettuce.

". . . in our Alaskan depot . . ."

Alaska! I don't even know where that is, but the psychologist says I should validate her adulthood and celebrate her choosing her own path. The daffodil in the vase wilts a little.

". . . has been approved," says Iris, gloating.

My eyes water from the bitter wine. I should smile. If I appear happy for her, perhaps she will eat the sandwich. I order a doggy bag. Napkin, our Wiener hound, will lick my hand tonight.

Bassoon Lesson

My battered Ford Escort rattled along the Hartbeespoort road.
The new American bassoonist in the National Orchestra had
recently moved in on Uranium Street, near the dip in the valley with
the trickling spruit. I crossed the low bridge where wait-a-bit thorn
trees grew and brand new houses had been set about the brown veld
overnight. Swimming pools glittered like aqueous kidney beans
in the barren earth awaiting roll-on lawns.

I arrived in a cloud of dust for my lesson. My teacher ushered me
into his kitchen. I unpacked my bassoon on the table beside a bowl
of apples, slinging the crook into the bell, before pouring a tumbler
of water for my reed. The centripetal force in the glass spun the
submerged reed in a whirling water ballet.

"Not that way," he chided. "You've too much water. An inch
is enough. Soak only the blades so you don't wet the binding."

I stepped into the sunken lounge to fetch his music stand, and
was startled by a soft hissing behind me. I spun around to a small
cobra reared up on the stair regally, its brown hood flaring. "Oh,
look!" I cried out in surprise, feeling honoured by its visit, if a little
afraid. It stared, swaying, then slithered behind the fridge where it
hid for the rest of the lesson.

At my next lesson the American told me he'd drowned the snake
in the swimming pool.

"You didn't have to do that," I said.

"I surely did," he said. "I'll have you know my lovely wife is
pregnant. I don't want no Affercan cobra hissin' 'bout my unborn
child. It took me four hours to kill the dumb critter. I pinned it
down in the leaf skimmer, but ever time I thought it must be dead,
it wriggled back to life. Just like Lazarus. Stupid serpent."

I spat out my scales in tight staccato triplets, barely able to
contain my disgust. He taught me about the Bible too, that
American. "See?" he said. "These sections printed in red are the

words our Holy Lord spoke directly."

"Did Jesus bleed his words, or did he just speak them?" I asked, wondering whether snakes have red blood too.

"Now you mind your mouth, young lady, or I might have to spank you."

I blushed feeling my ears redden.

"You'd like that, wouldn't you?"

I blushed, harder. Was his lovely wife also turned on by such talk. He was very knowledgeable about sin, that bassoonist.

I wanted to tell him that snakes' reflexes remain active for hours after death. Instead I told him that in Africa, we eat missionaries. He liked that notion, but oh, how I regretted shouting out when I saw that little snake. If only I'd stayed calm, or said, "Oh, while you're here, you should see how the eddies of the Sand Spruit join the Braamfontein Spruit at Witkoppen." The snake could have glided out while we chatted. I'd have watched from the corner of my eye while I told how the river winds westward from the Jukskei, into the Crocodile River that has no crocodiles, passing through Hartbeespoort Dam. I'd have expected no reptilian gratitude. I'd have marvelled at its subtle beauty as I described the Marico River that finally reaches the Elephant Child's grey-green greasy Limpopo all set about with fever trees.

For many nights afterwards I dreamed about the snake I'd betrayed.

He taught me a lot, that bassoonist. Mostly about scraping reeds and the sins of the flesh. "Kissing," he said, "strengthens the muscles of the embouchure."

Thorn

Josh wrote 'mortician' beside First Choice on the career guidance form. Mrs Kirk, the Life Orientation teacher, retrieved the forms she'd use to assist the Grade Nines in choosing their subjects for matric. Josh had not written down a second or third career choice. The form had not been signed by a parent or guardian.

When Mrs Kirk phoned his father, he said 'mortician' was wrong. He told her to put 'soil science', 'viticulture' and 'land management' on the form. He wanted his son to do a BSc Agriculture majoring in Oenology, at Stellenbosch University. Josh was to follow him in managing the family's wine farm, he said.

Jesus had given Josh a thorn from his crown to carve a message on his forearm: 'Oh Death, where is Thy sting?' The thorn didn't scratch out the words properly. It tore at his flesh, leaving only ragged lines. The teacher bent close to Josh, checked his eyes for redness or glassiness. His pupils were not dilated. She inhaled deeply, trying to catch the scent of sweet smoke on his clothes or hair. Nothing. Yet the boy was agitated. Adolescents, she shrugged. The teacher couldn't see the blood spots on Josh's sleeve, hidden under his blazer.

Josh borrows a grafting scalpel – the one his father uses to graft vine clones onto well-established rootstock. Perhaps it will work better, more precisely. Josh prays, asking forgiveness for spurning the Saviour's thorn.

He also borrows his father's hunting rifle

Bridgework

"Did you have a good rest yesterday?" asks Dr Lipkin tucking his
sideburns under a disposable mask. My husband, Johan, is his first
appointment on a Monday – the emergency slot.

Johan lisps, "I did not."

Yesterday afternoon, immediately after visiting the cheirologist
at the Healing Fayre, he spat out his bridgework in a mouthful
of toffee apple. Johan saved it, wrapped it in a paper serviette.
The dentist examines the mangled remains of his former colleague's
work with an inscrutable face. Bits of tissue paper have snagged
in the wire. Dr Lipkin scratches under his yarmulke with a well-
manicured finger then pulls on latex gloves. He looks about 19 years
old. This worries me about the most recent addition to the Norwood
Medical Centre. My husband also has well-manicured fingers,
but no yarmulke.

"Do you not rest on the Sabbath?" asks Dr Lipkin.

"I do not."

"My husband is a church organist," I say.

I do not explain that he is also a solitary Wiccan with Pagan
leanings – or a solitary Pagan with Wiccan leanings. Johan explained
the difference, but it passed through my agnostic head. Nevertheless,
he does not want it advertised to the charismatic evangelical
community he serves weekly at the pedals and console.

Johan believes that the taps leak when the water sprites feel
disrespected and that the tsunami was caused by the angering
of Jormungand, the world serpent that lies at the bottom of the sea.

"Those crazy Americans are trying to slay Jormungand.
Their military testing of secret eco-weapons on the seabed has caused
cosmic imbalance," he says, staring at the moon.

My husband lights green candles in the bathroom to appease
the spirits. There's no point explaining that the taps leak because the
council engineers were fixing the pipes up the road and the water

pressure changed. Last time the taps leaked, it was because
the washers needed replacing. I arranged for the plumber to arrive
while Johan practised with the church choir.

"Those green candles did the trick, didn't they?" he asked,
beaming. Yesterday he lit blue candles because it was Sunday,
or because he wished to astrally project prophetic dreams for healing
the ozone layer. Maybe it's just the summer solstice and he is casting
enchantments for truth, honour, loyalty and tranquillity upon our
house.

"Hurry up," says the dentist to his assistant. "You keep our
patient waiting."

The assistant is also new, demure in heavy woollen stockings
and a long skirt. She wears a snood and has wide frightened eyes.
She bumps the tray of tools beside the headrest.

"Easy does it, haste makes waste," grumbles Dr Lipkin. "What's
the rush?"

Johan meets with the new pastor once a month for coffee at the
Mugg & Bean. Pastor Frank told him at their recent meeting that
the Tsunami was a test of faith, and after all, faith in God can move
mountains and divide oceans. Johan told me that he didn't think
the minister would hold truck with Jormungand, so he said nothing
about the ancient reptile and muttered, "Uh-huh . . . Ja . . . I guess
you're right."

Then Pastor Frank asked Johan what he had been reading.

"Nothing," said Johan, lying through his dodgy bridge. The stack
of literature on his bedside table includes *Faerie Magicke, Runic
Script,* and *Wicca for You.*

"I've got just the book for you," said the pastor, pushing *Right
Answers for Wrong Beliefs* across the table. Johan thanked him and
returned last month's *Daily Devotion for Modern Believers* unread.

"How did you like it?"

"The wife enjoyed it," said Johan, lying some more. This satisfied
the pastor.

"Hallelujah, brother, what an answer to prayer!"

My wayward soul is high on Pastor Frank's list of spiritual

21

concerns. When he phones to book Johan for a funeral, and I answer the phone, he asks me how my walk with the Lord is going. I sigh and say, "Well enough Pastor," then yell for Johan before he asks about my return to the flock.

Johan said that when the cappuccinos and lemon meringue arrived, Pastor Frank stretched across the table to hold hands. He closed his eyes, and thanked the Lord loudly for His mighty blessings and pledged divine protection over their every step, trusting the precious blood of Jesus to guard them as they celebrated His abundant mercy.

The first time this happened Johan also closed his eyes and mumbled, "Amen" at every cadence. Today he stared at the mint leaf stuck in the cream and slipped silent incantations to the Goddess beseeching her forbearance of this necessary employer-employee ritual. Mint is a wonderful cleanser of the aura. Johan planted a sprig of it under the dripping tap in the garden.

This morning, I drove him to the dental surgery because he was muggy with pain. I was muggy with the thought of what his bridge cost in the first place. The dentist's former partner was a real number: a Bulgarian sadomasochist who wore thigh high white leather boots with her white mini and doctor's coat. I figured she had a matching black pair for her nocturnal pursuits.

We'd receive astonishing bills that charged for anaesthetic she'd never administered. When I queried the account, she'd deny giving only one of the four ampoules listed. I run my tongue along the uneven crowns I probably never needed and damn her to hell. Where were Johan's psychic powers when we let such a person loose on our teeth? Couldn't the angel cards have cautioned us against a tooth quack?

It was no big surprise when she was arrested for defrauding the Medical Aid and struck off the register.

After the first injection, the dentist rests his hand on my husband's shoulder. The assistant adjusts the paper bib.

"Hang in there, my brother," he says. Johan nods. "I bear no grudge against church organists."

Siyabonga Means Thank You

We've been waiting outside the indigenous nursery at the Kirstenbosch Botanical Gardens for half an hour with the new maid. She started last month. Her name is Siyabonga, which means 'thank you' in Zulu. I wish I had not lost my hat.

The sun is so bright reflecting off the page that I can hardly see to write the new journal I got for Christmas. Mom is inside ordering Waterwise plants with Raphaella, the landscape designer. Our old garden has too many exotic plants. They must go. All except the roses. Raphaella says it is fashionable to be environmentally responsible. Roses take a lot of water. You shouldn't waste water.

It's a precious resource.

When Raphaella saw us all in tow, she said, "Ag shame! They'll have a bit of a wait, hey?"

Mom said, "No prob, the maid will watch them."

We're Proudly South African now, so we buy stuff made here. Even plants. Proudly South African labels have a large tick in the colours of the new South African flag. The sun hats we bought at Woolies this morning had the tick. Corné and I argue whether it was a Chinese import that got the 'Made in South Africa' label when it got here or whether it was genuinely made locally. I read about that in the newspaper. She says it's a lie. Either way, Mom will be mad because mine is gone.

Today is so hot it seems the whole of Devil's Peak will ignite. All those oily plants heating up under the sun and no rain for ages. Our teacher says that the hole in the ozone layer is changing weather patterns around the world. There are water restrictions again this year, so Speed isn't allowed to use the hose. He's the garden boy who clears the leaves from the driveway with the hose, spraying a channel that gushes down the storm water drain. It takes ages while he talks to all the passers-by. Dad said it's lucky he wasn't called Lethargy.

Mom gave Siyabonga three tens and told her to buy us cold

drinks. That's not enough for five drinks. I said Siyabonga could have mine, but she wouldn't take it. I wanted to offer her a sip but it's not nice to drink from the same can. So I didn't. Mom said maybe she has AIDS because she was sick last week. Corné said, maybe she has 'flu. Mom says this country's going to the dogs; she says we should leave. Dad says we'll be here to turn out the lights.

Yesterday we saw a helicopter diving down into Hout Bay with a great bucket swinging and dripping. It swooped back up Chapman's Peak and sloshed the water over the burning mountainside. Can you get AIDS from sharing a can?

Corné's new cell phone has a camera. She bought it with her pocket money. She takes my picture and sends it to Mom. Then she texts: "We waiting, we waiting, it's getting aggravating."

Boykie and Renier start chanting the rhyme. When they start to kick each other in time Siyabonga says, "Come guys, let's find tadpoles." She takes them to Lady Anne's Bath, a bird-shaped pool that flows out and down through a shady glade. Lady Anne would not have known back in 1800 that soap pollutes the mountain streams. Corné says it wasn't her bath-bath, more like a swimming bath. It's too small to swim in and the water is cold. Coins thrown into the bath for good luck glitter dully in the half-light.

Corné asks for the change from the Cokes. Siyabonga holds her hands up, empty. "Then we can't make a wish," says Corné. Boykie is scooping tadpoles in his cupped hands and squealing as they wriggle away.

A notice in the loo warned against taking tadpoles home. It is cruel to animals. I'm not sure Siyabonga has read it. Come to think of it, I doubt she can read. Mom used to write the list of chores in a book for the last maid: polish the stoep, defrost the freezer, dinner party – 14 settings. Mom doesn't do that anymore. She tells Siyabonga what must be done, and then asks, "Got that?" Siyabonga repeats the list back to her: polish the stoep, wash windows, cook bobotie for supper.

Corné and I return to the bench, taking photos of each other. When Mom and Raphaella return, Mom's face is flushed. When we get in the car, she'll complain that she spent a bomb.

"Siyabonga took the boys to find tadpoles. They were grating our nerves," says Corné, rolling the 'r' for added emphasis.

Mom pats Raphaella's sleeve and says, "That woman is just the most divine maid."

"You're lucky. It's so difficult to find a good girl these days."

"Mine," says Mom, "is a gem."

Text

My editor sister goes to lots of book launches. She emails me the invitation to Penguin's launch of *Number Four*. It's the story of how the Old Fort, where Nelson Mandela was incarcerated during the Rivionia trial, was transformed into the new Constitutional Court. Three judges will talk at the launch. I should go. I don't know enough about my country's history, about the struggle. That embarrasses me.

She emails me half an hour later to say that her boss is sending her to a talk at Wits University instead. I must decide whether to go alone. The food is usually decent at these functions and if I go, I won't have to cook for myself. The music might be good too – African Jazz probably – although at the last function I attended, the guitar was out of tune and I couldn't leave because I was stuck in the middle of the row, next to Fr Michael Lapsley, who had both hands blown off in a letter bomb three months after Mandela's release. The priest held his teacup with a metal clasp that extended from below his shirt cuffs and I struggled not to stare.

As I get into my car it starts raining, heavy plops that bounce on the windscreen. A text message bleeps in pocket and I check it when I stop at a traffic light: *Traffic = living hell. Stay home. 40 min to reach Wits.*

I'm already on the road and hungry, so go a different route. My glasses have a raindrop on the lens. I rub it with the sleeve of my synthetic fleece jacket and it becomes a greasy smear.

At the Constitutional Court, the wind blows me up the forty-five steps from the parking lot to the table outside the Court. The first table has wine and juice, but I've quit alcohol and it's too cold for juice. There's hardly any food left. I grab a cold mielie but it's been cooked on an open flame and burned. The corn pits stick in my teeth, but I'm too hungry to put it down.

There are half eaten remnants of bread, but I don't take any, because I'm afraid of contracting hepatitis from the street people that frequent these launches. Peanuts and pumpkin seeds roasted without salt don't hit the spot either. The man beside me slurps from his wine glass and goes for a refill. Steam is rising from a big pot, but can't tell in the dark what it is. I hold out my hand to receive an enamel mug of what I hope is soup, hoping for a dumpling from the bottom of the pot.

I pass through a security arch. The enamel mug sets off the alarm. I have to go back through the arch without the mug. The dumpling in better light is an orange slice and the soup is gluhwein. I'd debate about getting tanked because there's no music and I'm lonely here without my sister, but I'm too scared to drive drunk in the rain.

I lose the gluhwein and head for one of the few remaining open seats on a low wooden bench that looks none too comfortable. The armchairs have been taken. My back hurts where the physiotherapist mashed it this morning. As I sit I'm stabbed by the sour smell of unwashed humanity.

Behind me is a balding youth with greasy hair hanging limply to his shoulders and big brown eyes, like Osama Bin Laden. He looks haunted. The venue fills quickly. I scout for other seats but there are none. I shift my scarf higher to cover my mouth and nose, but the benefit is minimal. Three elderly women perched on the bench behind him look like African queens in their traditional embroidered dress and turbans. They complain about the smell, tell him to move. He looks frightened, but stays put.

I put my cell phone on silent and return my sisters' message: *Too late. Am seated too close to noisome homeless dude. Food not up to much. Talk starting late. Hall cold. Hungry & cranky.*

I wonder why I came, hoping the judges are worth listening to. My sister sends another back to me: *The pungent indigent w soulful eyes steals. Watch your stuff. 16 car pile up on M1. Speaker 30 min late.*

I can't stop giggling. People sit on the steps, on the floor. A row of kids on the bench do not give up their seats to adults. I am uncomfortable about sitting on the bench when old people are sitting on the steps, but my back is too sore to relinquish my seat and there are no painkillers in my bag.

Albie Sachs talks first. An apartheid bomb blew off his one arm. He talks about an American who advised the building committee, but I don't follow what he says because when he gestures with both arms, his stump waggles in his cut-off sleeve. My mind wanders to the discarded cloth of his sleeve. Where is it now? And where are the remains of his limb?

The next speaker called to the podium is Johan Kriegler, the elderly man sitting beside me on the step. I am deeply embarrassed. He talks about the ghosts that haunt the place. He says the weather is a suitable reminder of those who died here. The Constitution has changed. The 'little people' have protection now. I look at the homeless man who has not been chased off by the intimidating grannies. I should have offered the judge my seat.

The last judge is Yvonne Makgoro in a vivid green dress and turban. She was a political prisoner, jailed alongside women guilty of Pass Law violations, guilty of loving across the colour line. She talks about her pain at returning there. The women who were imprisoned with her stand and sing. Their voices rise to hover and echo in the vaulted chamber. I wish I understood the words.

Before I leave, I try to buy a postcard to send to my sister in Manchester. It's impossible to tell her what happened here tonight. Ten postcards wouldn't be enough. As it happens, there are none for sale.

Ashram

It was not happy food we ate that first week we arrived: stale pumpernickel the colour of prunes; cheese with fur and bad breath; water only, neither juice nor hooch; and stringy pieces of meat that looked like boiled scarf and tasted like braised boot.

"Stop looking miserable," said Don, looking spiritual.

"I can't eat this food," I said, twisting the stalk off a tired apple.

I followed Don here with a different hunger. Now it's the wine of his kisses I thirst for. My yearning, which once he celebrated, is now a blemish between my thighs. When I sit on the bench against the dryer in the laundry, the warmth and vibrations ripple my flesh, loosen my longing. It starts at my feet, unlocking a memory that travels upwards to my emptiness. It doesn't leave, that yearning for the sky at my back, the earth at his, and the whole of heaven singing where we conjoined.

"We are here for love of the light," he reminds me when I refuse to talk. His smile transcends suffering. His lips have grown full. "Joy should sparkle from your very teeth," he says. But my gums are swollen and my tongue dry. "We are servants of the soul, foot washers."

I kneel before him, bending to kiss his instep. He loved it before when I sucked his toes, but now he pushes me away, saying, "We must wait for the guru. No blessing can be stolen."

My nails crumble and scabs won't form. His hair is long now and it shines on his shoulders, a glossy halo, blacker than feathers. Mine is falling out. There are bare patches on my scalp. Each morning I hold another tuft, greyer than yesterday's, twisted through my fingers.

Each night I lie awake. My bones are too pointed to sleep, the too slim mattress densely packed with skeletal women, sighing in their sleep. I fall out the bed, tumbling over the floor. I pass through the door and into the guru's chamber. I writhe past Don's slippers beneath the guru's bed and out, under the fence, down the hill. I roll all night under bumpy stars, over dark fields and black rocks, knocking off the last of my hard edges until I am small and shiny, round as a pebble.

In the marketplace at dawn I come to rest beside a clown. He picks me up and claims me as his own. From his wig he pulls a fat ripe banana, peels it back with dainty fingers, dips it in brown sugar conjured from his hat, saying, "Open your mouth for happy food. Eat up, eat up. You're too tiny, too thin." And I open my mouth to his sweet banana. Small as I am, I gobble it down. "More," he says. "Take more." I swell to the size of his other juggling balls

Gobble and swell; gobble and swell.

Spider Salad

A woman with big hair sidles in at the table next to us. Neo Freedom stares at her breasts nestling like a pair of ostrich eggs under a sweater the colour of winter grass, but I stare at the grey and shimmery spiders crawling all over her chest. I wonder why she does not scream, but she hasn't noticed them.

"No staring," says my mother, touching my cheek. I have practised eating with a knife and fork all week. But my hands are slow, and I'm not hungry. While the woman orders her food, a spider climbs off her sleeve and onto the tablecloth and then edges up to and onto the waiter's trousers while he writes her order in his notebook. I try not to stare, but I can't help following the spider that creeps up and down the waiter's leg.

Neo Freedom elbows me, saying, "Knock it off. That staring stuff is rude, okay?"

The waiter has breasts even though he is not fat. I wait for him to flick the spider off his pants, but the spider does not bother him. I am afraid that when he passes me, the spider will jump on me. I pull away when the waiter comes to take our order.

"Ease up," says Mom.

"Chill, chill, Chickiepop," says Neo Freedom, patting my hand before he uncurls my fingers to remove my knife and fork from my grip. To Mom he says, "Did she refuse her meds again?"

"Hush!" says Mom to Neo Freedom. Why is it rude to stare at strangers when it's fine to talk about your sister in the third person while she eats for the first time in a fancy restaurant?

"What can I offer my lady today?" says the waiter to my mother. She points to the frittata on the menu because she doesn't know how to pronounce it. The waiter writes '43' on his pad, mouthing the numbers as he does so. The spider watches me from the waiter's elbow. It wears velvet feathers on its abdomen.

"And what will the young master have today?" he says to Neo

Freedom, who wants the woman at the next table. He looks at the spider lady, licking his lips. The waiter nods and winks.

"A burger and fries, well done, and double-thick chocolate shake," says Neo Freedom.

"Good choice," says the waiter, scribbling in his notebook with his mouth still open. Then he looks at me and asks, "And what for the young missie?"

I want to ask for egg salad, but the only word to come is, "Spider, spider, spider . . ."

Perfect Timing

Marja unstrung her violin in anticipation of its repair.
She informed the orchestra's management of the hairline crack just
behind the fingerboard. She removed the violin from its black velvet
bed and laid it on Stan's workbench. Its nut-brown body looked like
a nude girl resting in the sun.

When she first saw the extended solo in *Temporal Salutation,*
the newly commissioned symphony composed by the resident
conductor's toy boy, Marja decided she was too old for ridiculous
virtuosity. Triple-stop harmonics, cross-string arpeggios, left-hand
pizzicato were a sight for sore tendons. Rhythmic shifts between
every conceivable time signature made her sigh. Marja was not one
of those leaders who thought herself indispensable; besides, it would
wear out her testosterone patch.

The timing was excellent. Marja's left hand was taking strain;
chiefly, her ring finger. She needed a break. With Clive, her new
lover. She blessed her late husband. She blessed the contract he had
drafted for her, stipulating that she would perform only on her own
Stradivarius.

"A crack in the varnish?" asked Stan, running his fingertips over
the surface.

"One that will take a whole month to fix," said Marja in her most
authoritative tone.

It was the perfect work for her deputy to present his virtuosic
ability to the world. Raoul was just like the piece – athletic,
muscular, aggressive. She could bank on his intention to steal the
maestro's new toy boy.

Raoul would play the solo with dedicated lust while she lay naked
on the beach, a nut-brown Madonna, receiving temporal salutations
of another kind. She would lead Clive into new territory for a
month. She wouldn't be missed. Her left hand ring finger would
probably recover.

Cell

My twelve-year-old son sleeps in his father's house twelve nights
a fortnight. At dawn he MXits me a message.
- *mornin ma. howd u sleep?*
- *I dreamed I set a bag of evil secrets on fire.*
As his words burst into my day, onto my screen, I recall the curve
of his thumb pressing, imagine him stretching, still in bed.
- *ooh sounds pretty bad*
- *This woman I knew was into corruption. She burned all*
her records.
What mysteries of ether? I bless the beautiful electrons, the cyber
ciphers that stoke me.
- *serious?*
- *Whoosh! We used the whole woodpile, nearly burned down*
the house.
- *i dreamed 2 but it was really long nd really strange.*
It can't get better than this. If he slept each night in my house
would we whisper so tenderly while he knotted his school tie?

Zebra Teeth

Two weeks before Petronella's birthday, Pa, who never read *The Star*, began scanning the classified section.

"We can't afford lessons," snapped Ma.

Pa dialled a number, muttering that he'd teach her himself.

Whatever he wanted was always gone already or too expensive by the time he got through. Ma bit her nails. Our butchery in Mogale City was doing badly.

"Petronella might like a canary . . ." suggested Ma, but Pa continued his mysterious quest. ". . . She needs another orthodontic plate."

Pa called Silas and Josiah to the bakkie one afternoon. "Shouldn't you hire professional transportation?" asked Ma as the men lit their hand-rolled cigarettes. "Those things are heavy! We can't afford for you to pop a hernia."

We trekked over a bumpy road near Potchefstroom, arriving at a farmhouse where a zebra skin lay underneath the jade velour couch with wagon-wheel armrests. Pa's rough hands stroked the piano's keys with reverence.

First he played a jolly rendition of *Jan Pierewiet*, then the tender *Sarie Marais*. When he'd finished *My Hart Verlang na die Boland* we drank bittersweet moerkoffie with the farmer. Pa haggled another hundred off the price before we heaved the piano onto the bakkie. Silas fed the thick rope through the loops and Josiah strapped it firmly against the cab with taut knots.

"Hold tight," shouted Pa from inside the bakkie as he started the engine. When he hit a donga in the dark the piano's lid flew open and all its cracked ivory teeth popped out. Silas shrugged. Josiah scratched his beard. I wondered as we jiggled and bounced along in the dark whether zebras ever needed braces.

She Cannot Love Her Own Air

After Samson Zambonelli has unpacked his oboe in the orchestra pit and soaked his reed, he takes out his wedding photos from his oboe case and shows them to Indira.

She glances through the photos, trying to smile. She studies the excess of rouched satin on his black bride, the puffed popcorn sleeves on chubby arms, and takes no pleasure in observing that the woman looks like a wedding cake. She wonders if he had to pay lobola. How many cows for a diva?

Samson's bride is a final year opera student with a voice like melted chocolate, and a moustache. Indira had warned her that marriage to an oboist would be hell: the bleating will keep you awake at night, causing exhaustion and resentment, and everyone knows that leads to infertility. Now Indira wonders whether she really said that. Maybe she just said, When he's fiddling with his reeds for hours, scraping, scraping with reamers and blades, you, my sister, will be driven to the axe. Maybe Indira just looked at the soprano and wished a family suicide upon her neck.

The soprano did not back away. She'd walked up close to Indira in the cafeteria line between rehearsals, waving her burger, saying in a fake American accent, "You be freaky all you like but he my man, my Sam, my Zam."

Indira had arrived at the School of Music on a scholarship, the top high school wind player in Limpopo. Samson taught her every week in the music rooms overlooking the jacarandas. She heard him tell her she would play like a deity one day, if she could just get the metaphysics.

"Go inward to your eyelid," he said, and Indira closed her eyes, exhaling. "Go deeper, down your neck, into your belly, lower, into your womb." She remembered her biology textbook: black and white line drawings in two dimensions.

"Be still as the veins of the rocks at the bottom of a well."

She didn't flinch. "Listen for the sign," he said. "Blow when you feel it." She waited for the feeling, for the knowing, but all she felt was empty, flat as a page.

Zambonelli spoke the words, never touching her, never adjusting a single finger, never meeting her gaze. He'd sit behind her in lessons, where she couldn't see him. He never even took his own oboe from its black case lined with burgundy velvet.

"Try," he said, "to follow the pattern of your longing." Indira tried, but her longing was with the condom in her handbag.

"I do, I am," she said, turning around in her chair to see him behind her. He was looking out the window, stroking his beard.

"Be still," he said without looking at her. She closed her eyes, saw the patterns of blood vessels, flickering after-images, but her sound stayed small and clipped.

Zambonelli taught her to make vowel sounds at the back of her throat. "Open your throat, open your heart," he'd say. "To play great music you must find the fractured parts in your dark places, so the whole can emerge in the light."

She closed her eyes again and sensed the grooves between her toes and toenails, the dry skin at the back of her knees, her moist armpits.

"Enter your darkness."

She thought of the folds of her silk. That dark place contained her hunger, her grovelling. Her organs had tightened, her lungs diminished. When she positioned the reed and blew, her sound trailed to nothing.

Her first oboe teacher, Miss Watkins, used to pat her shoulder if she hunched. She'd curved her palm over Indira's fly away fingers, bringing them home to the key pads, to the holes. Miss Watkins would tilt Indira's chin, guide her elbows. She would reach for Indira's diaphragm, holding Indira's own hand pressing it into her abdomen.

Zambonelli said, "Bring the sound from your feet to your teeth; feel it resist against every bone, right to your tongue, your gums, then give it way."

A cavity opened inside Indira's heart, resonating in her veins. Even the roots of her teeth, deep in her gums, filled with longing for his touch.

For ten years Miss Watkins had tapped the rhythms with a pencil on the music stand. She'd made Indira clap the phrases, then sing them, until they were precise and clean. She'd diagrammed the reed's shape, teaching Indira how to scrape the cane so that it was solid and reliable. She explained the diaphragm, the angle of the jaw, the curvature of a hand's position. "It's physics and mechanics," she'd said. "Think like an engineer: the speed of your air through the aperture defines the sound."

The conductor raises his baton. The soprano is on stage. Zambonelli smiles. Indira imagines Zambonelli licking butter and salt from his bride's roly-poly folds. Her tears come, but there's no tissue in her oboe case. She wipes her eyes with her pull-through, moist still from cleaning her oboe after her last lesson, when Zambonelli said, "Love your own air. Be unafraid."

She'd told the soprano that an oboist should marry an oboist, but the soprano, serene as the Black Madonna, stroked her belly in slow circular motions, as if reassuring the baby she was carrying that the world was not, after all, a crazy place.

Indira sits beside Zambonelli, watching him prepare each entry by the dim pit lights. She breathes with him, places her tongue on her reed at the exact moment he places his tongue on his own reed. From her feet to her teeth, the sound resists being given away. Even though they blow together, her breath moulded to his and the sound is bold and bright, she cannot love her own air.

Clutter

A large ceramic jar lingers in the corner, near the kitchen sink.
Because its sides were raised too fast, it warped in the kiln and has
an elliptical shape. It was a farewell gift from a student who was
no better as a potter than as a pianist. His scales jarred: uneven,
speeding off-balance. The stoneware glaze is a grey-green sludge,
the colour of the pustules that erupted weekly on his neck. No doubt
about it, the jar harbours bad energy, says my neighbour who runs
the Feng Shui consultancy.

Nail clippers with a broken spring, a gift from my ex-husband;
Thebe coins from Botswana, no longer in use; valueless Zimbabwean
dollars I can't discard, because I cannot bear to think of friends who
disappeared; the children's milk teeth deposited by the tooth mouse;
stale peppermints; unsolicited business cards; and a rusting safety pin
on a frayed red ribbon from the school sports day I left early because
I hated being a single mother. I'd cried watching my child come last.
And an almost completed course of antibiotics.

The student I taught badly, missed business opportunities,
the southern African trip that spelled the last days of my marriage,
the children's blighted infancy, my half-baked mothering and non-
compliance with doctor's orders – free-floating genies rise up, haunt
me when I do the dishes and stare at the jar.

I should throw it out. The jar and its contents. I want to but can't.
While the jar remains, some hope still lingers, a possibility that
I may yet become competent at something, some day.

I will buy a small bag of potting soil and tamp it down over the
teeth and pins, ribbons and mints, then mix in flower seeds and
water it. I will move it from the corner to the centre of the sunny
window. If I wait for long enough, the clutter below should dissolve
and if a chrysanthemum blooms, it will signify my absolution.

Epilogue for a Gun-Running Son

Hide your eyes, open your eyes, and see what Papa has brought for his baby.

Hide your eyes, open your mouth, and taste what Papa has bought for his baby.

The ancients warned of the second sighting in a two-moon month. Avert your gaze, daughter; they covered my curious child eyes in a game. Now there are no sweets, and still no father, but a sliver of ice at this first sighting. The summer's steam has chilled my living bones and my blood flows with stones and potshards, soldier son of my womb. The brittle red paint flakes, peeled from your boat, flow down the Zambezi into the sea. Hunger's lament was much kinder than this blue moon sorrow.

Row, row, row your boat, gently down the stream.

If you see a crocodile, don't forget to scream!

How you loved that song when I jiggled you on my back beside the tame spruit on the rough dirt track. Your high hollering, my best baby, made the grandmothers grin. Your blanket is empty now, like your boat they found, reported missing. Where was the action? Did you scream, son, when they came for you? Did you remember my play-play jaws that once clamped your chubby legs to make you laugh? We were hungry and your father gone. The laughter stilled our stomachs' rumble for a while. From the other side, can you row my still beating heart to the middle of the river? Feed it to a beast below, so the rest of me may join you soon.

One, two, three, four, five, once I caught a fish alive,

Six, seven, eight, nine, ten, then I threw it back again.

Kleintjie's Saint

Kleintjie September is already sitting on the rickety piano stool when Miss Marvel limps in. A smell of damp socks lingers in the room from the pipes that leaked through the roof in the long holiday. Nobody discovered the leak for weeks. Miss Marvel throws open the windows to let in a breeze. She rests her head on the burglar guards, inhaling the scent from a potted magnolia outside.

Kleintjie's toes don't reach the floor, so she swings her feet while fingering each black note from top to bottom. She curls one foot around the leg to reach the lower octaves, but wobbles, thumping both hands on the keys. Miss Marvel, who is sharpening her pencil, cringes at the dissonance.

Kleintjie's music book is dog-eared and dirty. At the last lesson Miss Marvel spent five minutes wiping squashed banana off the cover. Kleintjie opens to *When the Saints go Marching In*. A button has popped off her tight school uniform; her shoes are almost worn through. Her nose wants blowing and her hair is wild. Miss Marvel encircles one bird-like wrist gingerly in her old fingers. She turns Kleintjie's hand over and holds it up for the child to see.

"Duh! I forgot to wash."

"I see that," sighs Miss Marvel, catching in a whiff of peanut butter as Kleintjie dashes to the cloakroom. She returns with wet smears on her uniform. The music teacher suspects the girl ignored the soap as well as the towel, but the piano has been spared the worst of the playground grime.

"Did you have your lunch time pill?" Miss Marvel didn't check the secretary's medication register for Kleintjie's back-to-front K.

"Yes, Ma'am," she says, sniffing. Miss Marvel passes a tissue. Kleintjie blows her nose, jumps from the chair and knocks over the bin beside the piano. Pencil shavings and discarded papers spray over the carpet. "Clumsy cunt," says the child under her breath. Miss Marvel should respond. She ought to say something.

Anything, like, "Not that ugly word for my special girl." Or, "No name-calling at our school, Kleintjie." Instead she yawns loudly and pretends
not to hear.

"These curly-whirlies are stuck, Ma'am," says Kleintjie picking at the pencil shavings snagged in the carpet.

"Leave them now," says Miss Marvel, wishing the Grade Three class teacher had refrained from telling the head teacher how much music was helping Kleintjie.

Miss Marvel should march around the classroom, stepping behind her, to pat her shoulders in tempo, saying, "Left-right-left-right." It usually improves a wonky rhythm. Her hip is too sore and she is too old. Instead she says, "Easy girl, let's tap the pattern now. Ta ta ta ta-a-a-a-ah!"

They tap with two fingers and sing, "Oh, when the sta-a-a-ars begin to fa-a-a-all, oh, when the stars begin to fall . . ." But still, Kleintjie can't play the melody in steady time.

Mrs September arrives after each lesson, chattering happily. She tells Miss Marvel, "My daughter sings that song every day." Or, "She really loves her music." Or, "Kleintjie adores you, you know?" Miss Marvel forces a smile. She could kick herself for her aversion to the child who runs across the quad to hug her, bashing Miss Marvel's breasts with her woolly braided mop.

At the year-end tutor forum the head teacher announces the decision to keep Kleintjie September in mainstream education: "Kleintjie will not be going to the remedial centre after all. Thank you for your effort!"

The other teachers smile and nod their heads. Miss Marvel's hip aches. She limps up the stairs singing, "Oh, when the moo-o-o-o-oon turns into bloo-o-o-o-ood, oh, when the moon turns into blood."

Vanilla Silk

"Don't underestimate her." Madame Bettina's instant message flickered across my screen late on Monday afternoon. We were finalising arrangements for my first corrective therapy session.

"Sarah's vanilla all the way," I typed back from my university office.

"Doesn't mean she's stupid."

"Sure."

"She hasn't figured?"

"Nope."

On Tuesday a plain manila envelope arrived in the mail. I opened the contract unwittingly at the kitchen table, in front of my wife. My stomach clutched.

Terms of our agreement ... bound, gagged, caned ... restraint shall not be removed ... further correction required ... The safe word "vanilla silk" will indicate ...

Sarah stared at the envelope I held in trembling fingers. I whisked it away, stammering a feeble lie.

"How pale you look," she said, stroking me with cool hands. I caught a whiff of 'Happy', the sweet perfume she wore. I'd given her Dior's 'Poison', but she refused to wear it. "Too dark," she'd said.

Thursday's package contained a leather blindfold and six-inch heels. I blushed at the ivory lace thong, cream stockings and twelve-clip suspender belt. My legs bounced in uncontrollable agitation, my erection throbbed.

Undressing to meet my Mistress, I yearned momentarily to flee, to return to the safety of Sarah's toasted cheese sandwiches and our safe, seemingly-happy home. But once I'd slid my foot into the hose and adjusted the seams, I could not. A floral motif on the ankle matched the lace tops where the garters attached. I felt nauseous with anxiety, demented with desire. My dick swelled against the lace as I slipped the blindfold on and waited as instructed. My back to the door, arms behind me, I dared not turn towards her footsteps.

I surrendered to the click of handcuffs. As she opened my mouth to take in the rubber gag, an ominous whiff of 'Poison' filled the room.

"How pale you look," was all she said.

Prescription

Tanya crouches beneath the table, hidden by a long grey cloth. She sculpts soggy pasta leftovers into the crack in the floor, a gaping hole shaped like half a heart.

Sister Patel, who is pregnant, wears a headscarf and mutters prayers as she knits a striped sweater in bold colours of lamb curry, mango atchar, pimento relish, tandoori fish. Each stitch is a prayer for the soul of her unborn, a pink watermelon growing under her white uniform.

Every night the pasta plug has shrunk from the edge of the hole and fingernail slivers and strands of hair are embedded in it. Tanya removes the shrunken plug and drops her pills through the hole again, then makes another one with mashed potato or mushy peas, or white bread chewed until it's pliable. Now that she has stopped taking the pills, she has recovered her vision. She can see through the floor and walls again. She sees the fluttering of Sister Patel's baby with its malformed ventricle.

While Sister Patel casts on the cuffs of the baby sweater, Tanya removes the old plug, studying its half-heartedness. She slips into the smoker's lounge, and drops the plug into the hoary curtain where the lining has ripped. On her way back she whispers to Sister Patel, Keep saying your prayers, darling. That baby girl needs them.

Viola Practice

Jose's dimples had got lost among the scars and pustules that formed a waffle grid on his fat cheeks. He knelt meekly with his grandmother as she beseeched St Jude for a miracle every morning. He endured without complaint as she scrubbed his face with witch hazel each night.

When the girl who wore a diamanté G-string and sat next to him in the viola section poked him in the ribs with her bow because he was pushing the tempo in the adagio, he told her she was prettier than Kate Moss. She told him he could kiss her ass.

The next morning he got up half an hour early, poured the witch hazel down the drain, set St Jude on his brother's skateboard pointing downhill and tuned his viola with a different ear.

Waiting for the Lotto

Every Wednesday, the lotto jingle plays each hour on every radio station: "Tata ma chance, tata ma millions . . ."

Suzette Coetzer turns the radio down as her first class arrives. She bought a lotto ticket at the Athlone Quickshop when she filled up at the garage. It is hard to tell which will happen first – winning the lotto or the Good Hope Remedial Centre getting the promised payout. Both eventualities seem equally unlikely.

The class jostles in line outside the studio. Nyiko's crutch accidentally trips Mpumi. He scrapes his knee on the ground. Suzette dons rubber gloves to wipe the wound clean. It is the last pair in the box. There is no money left in petty cash for more.

"Thula, buti," she croons, opening the antiseptic and dousing a ball of cotton wool. She wipes gently around the cut. It's possible, but unlikely that he has AIDS. He doesn't have the pronounced pinched face.

The rest of the class are taking their places and start to fiddle with the tools on their desks. "No touching yet. You have to wait a moment. I'll be right with you."

Looking up from the gravel that is stuck in Mpumi's graze, she sees Nyiko dig his nails into the lump in front of him. "Leave it alone, Nyiko," she warns. As soon as her head is bowed again, Nyiko pinches off a piece and slips it into his mouth.

With a plaster on his knee, Mpumi hobbles to his desk with an exaggerated limp. The class has started late. Today they will make Mother's Day presents. Miss Coetzer instructs them to roll out their lumps evenly.

Suzette notices Nyiko drooling clay gravy as he rolls out his lump. His movements are slow, precise. He hasn't been assessed, because the centre can no longer afford an occupational therapist. His fine motor co-ordination was probably compromised by a birth injury. Or a blow (or blows) to his head. She wipes his face with a towel.

He wrinkles his nose, complains.

At the next table, the rolling pin thunks over the edge of Sipho's clay pat. On the radio the Soweto String Quartet plays *Zebra Crossing*, one of the station's standards. She likes the children to hear classical music. It calms them, but today the children wriggle and fidget more than usual. Sarah bumps the table, Nyiko grumbles. Suzette tells them to quit it.

"He started," says Sarah.

"Enough now. Have you cut your bird out yet, Sarah?"

Sarah holds the cut-out up for her teacher's inspection. It is too thin. The shape stretches and the girl flings it down on the board. "Don't fret, Sarah. Just start again," she says, rolling the clay back into a ball and handing it back to Sarah.

"Is that smooth enough yet?" Miss Coetzer asks Sipho, who adjusts his heavy spectacles. He squats with his chin resting on the desk, the clay level with his eyes and pats it.

"Yes, Miss."

"Good," says Miss Coetzer as she hands him a cookie cutter in the shape of a bird. She wipes away the crumbs of clay sticking to his moist chin. He presses the shape out of the cookie cutter and lifts the surrounding clay away from it.

"Inyoni!" He squeals with enthusiasm

"What is the English word for 'inyoni', Sipho?" the teacher asks.

"Bird?"

"Right," Miss Coetzer smiles. This is a breakthrough.

Sipho flaps around the class with lumbering wings, sends Mpumi's rolling pin spinning, which knocks Nyiko's pinch pot to the ground. Ten months ago she applied for funding from Uthingo. There is still no confirmation. She has made endless calls to disinterested clerks.

"Mampara! Clumsy fool!" shouts Mpumi, kicking Sipho with his good leg. Sipho retreats, cowering under the corner table. His teacher crawls in beside him, wraps her arms around the keening boy. The grant the centre receives from the Nelson Mandela Children's Fund barely covers the running costs. Very few parents can afford the fees.

"Settle, boykie, settle down." Sipho's heart hammers like
a trapped bird under his ribcage. She holds him and watches Nyiko
putting clay in his mouth again. Last week's headlines announced
the disappearance of Lotto millions. In the careers section there were
posts advertised for remedial teachers in the United Arab Emirates.

"Nyiko! Don't do that." She thinks of the newspaper headlines,
railing at the loss of South African teachers to British schools.
"Clay is not for eating. Spit it out." Nyiko swallows, grinning.
He will get worms, she thinks. Then: he probably already has them.

In the boot of her car is her change of clothes. She wants to
look suitably chic for the job interview this afternoon. Underneath
the table she does not feel sophisticated holding a frightened boy,
rocking in her arms. If only she could shower, could rinse away
the smell of sadness.

The health inspector will close the centre if an assistant is not
appointed by next term. Sipho quietens, then crawls from the nest
of her arms. She climbs out from under the table, feeling stiff.
She brushes clay dust from her knees and goes to inspect the other
children's birds.

"Good work, Mpumi . . . Make a hole for the hanging thread
now, Nyiko . . . Nice feather decoration, Sarah. You've tried hard."

Just before the class ends, the radio jingle plays again. "Tata ma
chance . . ."

Suzette Coetzer stares at the glossy leaflet she received from the
educational recruitment agency. In the foreground is a palm tree.
A child joins the voice on the radio, chanting, "Your license
to dream."

Behind the palm tree is a minaret.

State Theatre

It is Saturday in the State Theatre, and there's just enough time between the matinee and the evening shows of *My Fair Lady* to grab a sandwich. I used to be able to leave my bassoon in the pit, but instruments get stolen these days. It's too heavy to schlep around, so I hide the bassoon case in the shower stall in the change rooms.

Nobody showers here any more. Nobody even comes here. Pale ballerinas with pointy bones and blank faces used to. That was in the old days. We, the orchestra girls, would bustle past them in the shared amenity, feeling enormous. I was pregnant and the largest of all. My borrowed black maternity shift cut into my armpits; I was always plucking at the sleeves. When I refreshed my lipstick at the mirror, I'd peep sideways as the ballerinas peeled off their leg warmers and leotards, envious of their flat stomachs and spidery limbs.

In the canteen they used to buy apples and cigarettes. I'd order a hamburger and *slap* chips, blushing privately as I scraped up my pre-natal entitlement. And when I lugged the contrabassoon into the pit, I felt just as unbecoming as my cumbersome instrument. I hated its rude sound, like fat vibrating farts. Eating before I played gave me acid reflux.

When my baby was born I couldn't hear anything except his cries in my head, raucous as the hadeda ibis at dawn. In rehearsals I'd count the rests, take up my instrument, inhale, watch the conductor, play a note and wince. Too sharp. Or flat? I'd pinch my lips; bite harder. My principal scowled. I'd shake, lose my place, mess up the key changes, miss entries.

After my last performance I drove the hour home at midnight with full breasts, hoping my baby would feed. Walt Ledbetter growled on my radio: "My girl, my girl, don't you lie to me. Tell me, where did you sleep last night?" At home I banged my head against the tiled corner of the shower. My milk swirled, bluish, down the drain.

The next day I phoned the booker and said I'd call him once the baby was sleeping through the night. Then the orchestra closed down. It was 1994, and the new South Africa didn't want white men's music any more.

Twelve years later we're back, but the theatre looks shabby, with graffiti and broken soap dispensers. You have to bring your own toilet paper. The dancers are black girls now, hip-hopping in the elevators – robust, with hips and breasts and attitude. They eat Big Macs and their mobiles have kwaito ring tones, which they answer like American TV stars, shoulders swaying, fingers snapping.

In the pit, before the performance, the tall clarinet player beside me tucks one foot under his hugely muscled thigh and sucks his reed. His head is thrown back, eyes closed. I study his face, close enough to touch: receding hairline, full lips. I want to reach under his clarinet shielded against his chest, to feel his pecs, his abs. Instead, I practise the tricky solo in 'Why Can't The English?' The clarinet player opens his eyes, and says, "That one's a dog; try it slower." I do.

During the clarinet solo I watch his construction-worker's fingers moving over the keys. He catches me watching him and winks. I blush, imagining his fingertips on my collarbone, on my chin, moving lower. I want him to make me croon sweeter than his clarinet. I count the measures until my solo, wanting to kiss the fleshy pad of his thumb. He nods, offering me the cue. We breathe together and blow. His note above, mine bass to the chord. Later, when I play my own solo, the sound is pure and true. The clarinet player scrapes his foot on the floor, orchestra code for "well done".

On Sunday after the matinee, I will follow Mr Clarinet out the pit, whistling 'Wouldn't It Be Luverly?' I'll follow him to the canteen, then join him at a rickety table and sip a coffee while he rips the flesh off a chicken drumstick, wishing I was bold enough to lure him to my hiding place in the shower.

The Virtue of the Potted Fern

It's not easy to organise a bookshelf that's been moved from the guest room to your bedroom because your South African relatives are coming to stay. Skoonma is allergic to house dust mite. (The next entry in *Die Suid-Afrikaanse Skool Woordeboek* is 'skoonmaak' – to clean.) You should get a maid, is what she always says.

Prepare to be ruthless. You're working in the dark. And you write the rules for this activity yourself. Like the rules for entertaining foreign in-laws, they do not exist.

Keep *The Complete I-Ching* (this is fallacious – the nature of the oracle is open-ended) away from *Children Are From Heaven* (they're not). Do not mix *Healing Back Pain* with *The Story of O* (and do not – under any circumstances – try this in your own home).

Similarly, discourage contact between *City of Djinns* and *Learn to Speak Zulu*. The African and the Indian were never happy bedfellows.

Preferably, set *The Courage to Be Rich* apart from *Music in the Classic Period* (Beethoven perceives that Suze Orman has a tin ear) and specifically separate *The Wizard of Oz* from both *The Complete South African Health Guide* (references to tinnitus offend the tin man) and *The Kruger National Park* (this bothers the lion).

If you must, group *Conducting the Elementary School Choir* with *The Satanic Verses* and *The 30-Day Fat Burner Diet* with *Good-Bye to Guilt*. A modicum of tolerance may be temporarily exhibited. In contrast, it may seem logical to set *The New Oxford English Dictionary* beside *Noah Webster*, but the bickering will soon disabuse you of that notion.

Block your ears when you throw together *How To Talk So Kids Will Listen & Listen So Kids Will Talk*, *A Pacifist's War* and *The Importance of Understanding*. Disregard the howls of protest when you saddle Grisham's *Bleachers* with Coetzee's *Disgrace*.

Experiment with different combinations. Nothing is permanent.

However, multiple failed attempts to obtain satisfactory resolution should point you towards the monthly charity book sale held by the Deaf Education Centre. They will not be troubled by the raucous clamour, the untuned voices. Be practical. Persuade them to take the bookshelf too.

A potted fern by your bedside will prove a quieter option. Ignore peculiar looks when you take a stroll in the park with the plant tucked under your arm. Disregard the stares when you seat yourself on a public bench, perusing the ultimate in erotic literature, gently opening the dusty green leaves.

Decode the delicately furled spine. Consult the star signs in each powdered whorl. Translate the love letter tangled in the maidenhair. Finger each fiddlehead with a tender touch. Ponder its humble virtue.

Suspect

At first we thought Mel's switching words about was a new affectation, a verbal anarchy, like the garish make-up: orange eye-shadow, green lipstick, artificial eyelashes.

"She is trying to annoy," said my mother, rolling her eyes.

"She is trying to be hip," I said.

When I asked what she wanted for supper, Mel said, "Mash and fingers fish." When she told us about the "game blame" her father was playing I figured it was just the new way of being funky, like the odd twitch I thought I noticed in her face from time to time.

Before she left for a party last Friday, she appeared in a purple velvet gown from the Salvation Army shop, combined with the hiking boots she'd stolen from her step-mother, entering the room as if to hidden trumpets, like a monarch waiting for a lackey. I said, "Odd, Chickadee, you're the oddest sock I know, but a beautiful one anyway."

She hugged me and said, "I love you Mah-mi." My mother sniffed and raised her eyebrows.

After Mel had left Mom said, "You shouldn't encourage her. You really shouldn't." There was nothing deliberate about the jumbled sentences. Mel didn't even notice them.

Yesterday, while squatting in front of the book shelf, she asked, "Where is the Pages Yellow?"

I'd just switched off the blender and the whirring hadn't quite died down. I was sure I'd misheard. I called out: "What, what did you say?" She twitched, smiling like a convert to a beatific religion, and said, "Never mind, I got it."

She'd also started throwing up, suddenly and violently. Bulimia? No. She didn't try to hide it. She'd just had her period and her hand-washed panties had hung on the bathroom line, tampon dispensers wrapped in toilet paper were in the bin.

When she left for school, I looked under her bed, inspected her sheets for blood spots, I rifled through the jumble of underwear, scared of what I'd find, imagining needles, rolling papers, or strange granules. Blades. Pills.

I peeled through her garbage, but found only notes from other girls, gossiping about the teachers, about boys. In her stick-scratchy script she wrote: *Declan is a loser, Binky. Don't mind him.*

When, I wondered, did her handwriting get so messy? Binky's writing was all curves and bubbles, prettified hearts instead of dots above the 'i' in 'fuckwit' and 'dickwad'.

Under her bed was a Tupperware with a chicken mayo sandwich from last week and my best black lace bra, missing for three weeks, now grey with dust. I found gum wrappers and an elasticised ankle guard.

I switched on her computer, checked out her facebook page, found a friendship wheel, a fun wall, groups like "I Dont Care How Comfortable Crocs Are, You Look Dumbass".

I checked her recent history. She'd visited sites for games, one where you untangle a ball of knotted string, another where you poke out the teacher's eyes with flying pencils, land spitballs in her hair. Some You-Tube vids. The weirdest thing was a pop-up ad for sexy girls in Tembisa – all blonde and blue-eyed, looking like Swedes.

I checked her google searches.

I thought I'd see 'dagga' or 'ganja' or 'hash', but all I found was clues to her biology research: central nervous system, diurnation, abnormal prion protein, and hemodynamic imaging. She'd looked up her own name, her stepmother's, my own. Not inappropriate.

Last night she limped to the table. "What's with the foot, Kiddo?" said my mother. Mel stopped and cocked her head, staring at her grandmother as if she was speaking Zulu. Mom shot me a look suggesting that Mel was acting, playing for sympathy. "Melanie-Jane," she said, enunciating each syllable as if addressing an imbecile, "why are you limping?"

I thought Mel would storm out, flip us the finger but she straightened a bit and twitched, wincing. Mel patted her grandmother's shoulder in passing and said, "Up ease, Grandma.

Nothing wrong with my legs."

This morning she came home from school at 10 am, swaying slightly to one side as if carrying a heavy bag but all she had was her small khaki tote covered in graffiti. I wondered if she was bunking, if she'd been suspended.

I said, "Hey, Chickadee, what's up? You forget something?" My mother, speaking at the same time, said, "Have you hurt your knee? Did you twist your ankle? What's *wrong* with you?"

Mel kicked off her shoes, almost losing her balance, dropping the bag. She walked over and climbed onto the couch beside me, handing me a folded paper, snuggling into my lap. It was a print-out from a website, familydoctor.com. Another from selfdiagnosis.com.

"Hold this head, Mah-mi, please hold this sorry head."

Where is Boeta's Skedonk?

Last year there was a Ferris wheel on the empty lot outside Riebeeckstadt. Boeta and I stole raspberry kisses in the gondola, wishing it would stop – break down – with us midair, staring over the satellite dishes poking from the old warehouses below; vehicle tracking systems to recover hijacked trucks. Spun sugar fluttered from the candyfloss stall and popcorn kernels stuck in our teeth. Sober still, we sang like drunks. A year later three hundred pondokkies popped up, squished together on the ghosts of fairground merriment. Housing for the masses. Perhaps the previously disadvantaged are happy now? I reckon they might find Boeta's skedonk here. I look at a shiny tin roof, with a car tyre on it. Lightning protection. That's what the police captain told me. Is this what a hijacker's house looks like? I wish the Ferris wheel were here still. Maybe I would find Boeta in a gondola now.

Dusters

When Jack left Pretoria to go with his mother to London, his Ouma gave him a magic yellow freedom suit that gave him psychic powers. His mother said they were just pyjamas. One morning after they got to their new home, he sat at the breakfast table, twirling his Weetbix around his plate until it disintegrated.

While slurping the soggy mush, he made a grey parrot with red tail feathers out of plasticine. When he came home from nursery school, the neighbour's African Grey – which had escaped from its cage – was perched on his bedroom windowsill waiting to be let in.

One hot July morning at breakfast, he crafted a bus from the red modelling clay. Parp, parp! His bus hooted and chugged around a milky puddle that had slopped out the bowl. It ground to a halt in the traffic at the edge of the breakfast table. With a paring knife Jack sheared off the front of the bus at a peculiar angle, sliced its roof open at the midline, and flicked away a wheel. He rolled slivers of black plasticine into a disembodied foot, an arm, a headless torso.

When the floor jolted and the windows shook and a smell of burning filled the air, Jack smirked at his mother as if to say: pyjamas or magic yellow freedom suit?

Six months later he moulded a bottle-nosed whale the colour of dark minerals. When his mother turned the telly on, the news anchor announced the rescue effort underway in the Thames. His mother said it was time to buy new pyjamas.

The next day Jack made two plasticine people: the boy wore yellow pyjamas and an expression of sorrowful knowing. The mother's hair hung straight and brown down her back. Her dress, the colour of oatmeal, revealed a pregnant bump. While Jack was at nursery school, his mother used a home-test kit, then took out her scissors and snipped the magic yellow freedom suit into dusters.

Late

"Stop!" I yell, flinging my hands from the keyboard mid-phrase.

An electric storm is brewing and the fake shaving cream snow, which has been spray-painted onto the windows for the year-end party, intensifies the gathering gloom. Sizwe, who is usually alert, is silent and withdrawn today.

"Switch on the light. Perhaps you'll see the music better." The rain has come very late this year and although we are well into summer, the piano's keys are heavy with dust. I wipe my handkerchief over them while Sizwe trudges across the room to flick the switch.

The students have painted stylised holly and ivy bouquets on butcher paper and a giant cardboard Father Christmas for the backdrop of the stage. The red figure is slumped behind the piano, but a ghoulish grin protrudes over the top. I play the opening chords of the introduction, but Sizwe isn't listening. He enters a measure before the cadence.

"Too early," I say. Sizwe trails off, looking dejected. His flute sags on his shoulder. It is the third time he has missed a simple entry. "Again?" I ask. He nods, lifts his instrument and polishes the mouthpiece with his cuff.

Sizwe is seventeen, talented and a sponsored student. His parents are semi-literate casual labourers who live in the Diepsloot squatter camp. The year-end recital is a week away. Our first rehearsal with piano accompaniment is going particularly badly.

"Why do you keep ignoring the rest?" The rain smell blows through the classroom.

My student lives in a tiny shack with five siblings and elderly grandparents who share the accommodation. When he practises, the neighbours scream, "O a rasa!" You make noise.

During term, he leaves the flute in a locker and practises after school. The arrangement is not ideal, as he gets locked out the classroom I have arranged for his use if he's five minutes late. The cleaner, who is always eager to leave the premises early, was promised a nice Christmas box for his co-operation, but the pre-festive offerings of Old Brown don't do the trick.

"Were you unable to practise?"

He shakes his head, and says, barely audibly, "I practised."

I thought he'd be the highlight of the concert. I've invited guests from the Nelson Mandela Children's Fund to hear him. He should get a scholarship to Wits University.

"I don't understand. You've been playing so well . . ." A sudden gust of wind heralds the first heavy drops of rain and the music flutters off both our stands. I stretch out to slam the window and ask, "What is up with you?"

"Allegro," he says.

"Count carefully, okay?"

He nods. We try again. His sound is rich and round, his intonation perfect. I glance at him and stumble. His eyes glisten. The tricky spot approaches, I count aloud, "One-and two-and ONE . . . too LATE!" I lose my temper and shout, "You're late, dammit, late again!"

Late!

Awareness dawns. The euphemism. I shudder.

"This about Thandi?"

Tears well in his eyes. Thandi left school a month ago. We buried her in the hard earth at Avalon last weekend.

"Were you . . ." I hesitate, struggling for the correct word, "close?" He nods. A flash of lightning reflects along the length of his flute. "How close?"

He tucks his flute under his arm and loops his fingers together, in the unmistakable gesture of copulation.

I thunk my elbows down on the keys, clutch my head in my hands, groaning. I lay his flute on top of the piano, cradling his head against my chest, feel the grooves of his fashionable corn stalks under my hand. Rain thrashes against the window that doesn't close properly. The snow inside weeps milky trails, pooling on the dusty ledge below.

Can HIV be contracted through tears? I have no open lesions through which the virus might pass, just a hole in my heart the size of a teenager's coffin.

My Mother's Diary

The view from up here is incredible and makes me feel again.

This entry in my mother's diary is dated 26 May 1970. The pages are brittle and her script is girlish and square. She had to leave school in Standard Eight, but she continued reading books she borrowed from the library. These backward-leaning blocks of cryptic print are a tenuous link to the time of which she wouldn't speak. Or couldn't.

The straight ridge of Table Mountain, when seen from the highest point of the Lion's Head, is not as straight as when viewed from afar. The Castle, with its suffering ghosts, the rail tracks leading north to where my heart is, and the glittering vastness of False Bay, somehow diminishes my troubles. This vista even seems to diminish the troubles of this aching wicked land.

From the date of the entry, I know this is when she met Koos secretly. Yet there is no mention of him – only oblique references to the pickled fish that was his favourite food, which she had packed in the picnic basket. That detail would keep the memory alive for her, but would protect them both when the security police came to call on moonless nights.

A sugarbird alighted on a pincushion bloom, as I set out the snoek and boontjieslaai on enamel picnic plates. It seemed to gloat at the ease of its existence – the cheeky thing – as if to say, "Look how easily I am sustained here on the mountain . . . Come join me. Come, come!"

At the time, I was ten, mortified by my enormous breasts, and I didn't know of the existence of my mother's lover. The boys at Liesbeeck Senior Primary called me, 'Tits Tessa'.

"I'll give you fifty cents if you take off your top," said Hond, waving a shiny coin at me.

"One Rand if you take off your panties too," said Smous.

I ran home, blushing and crying. My mother sat motionless, staring into space. I couldn't tell her what the skelm boys had said.

If the mountain has witnessed atrocities and endured, it will surely

witness more and endure a little longer. I can survive this too, like my
mother, and my grandmother too. Like her mother and grandmother as
well. The lure of black female flesh is nothing new.

The first time the police arrived, I pissed myself. After they'd gone
I went to my mother's room to get fresh sheets. She lay in a huddle,
sobbing under her blanket. I crawled into bed with her. She was
wet. It wasn't just tears, but I didn't know it then. I fell asleep, curled
against her, and saw the blood the next day when she washed our
sheets and nighties in the zinc basin that stood in the back yard.

I hope they will spare my Tess . . .

The police came regularly, looking for Koos. I always wet myself.
One night they pulled me out of bed. The sergeant with big hands
laughed at my wet nightie.

"Such a big girl," he leered, fondling my breasts. "But still you
wet your bed, hey? Ag sies!" I yelped when he tweaked my nipples.
He said to my mother, "Will you speak when I take your daughter?
Will you?"

"Leave the kid alone," said the captain flipping through my
mother's diary. "You fixed the bitch?"

"Ja, Kaptein."

. . . . but they will not leave her be much longer. The poor child has
inherited my chest prematurely. I wish I had taught her better about
being a woman. My heart is too bitter.

The next day, my mother sent me with a neighbour on the train
to my grandmother in Beaufort West. A month later I heard my
mother was in jail.

There is one more page to this diary that miraculously escaped
confiscation. The earlier and later ones all disappeared. But I can
read no longer. I vomit suddenly and violently into the toilet and
wonder whether memories exhumed too rapidly can kill a person.
Afterwards, as I hold my mother's ashes in a plain cardboard box,
I start to feel a little calmer. I have not known where to scatter them.
I call a taxi, tuck my mother's diary into my backpack and direct
the cab driver up the windy street to the start of the footpath up
Lion's Head.

A little way along, a sugarbird darts and lands on a protea bloom. From the top of the mountain, the castle languishes below, the glittering rail tracks head north and the vista of False Bay spreads beyond.

I want to capture the scenery from up here. It's a matter of time before I disappear, either into my grave – which would be a blessed relief – or into a dank airless cell. I want to savour every strand of fynbos, to outline each cloud of the Tablecloth draping the mountain into my memory forever, to engrave the bright yellow of the sugarbird's long tail. Perhaps if I can hold onto the mountain to keep me sustained in the dark night that will surely come, I shall be a useful – maybe even good – mother to Tess.

I, too, begin to feel again as I release my mother's ashes to the wind, freeing her to join the sugarbird at last.

The Piccolo Blues

Candide. By Leonard Bernstein.

The flute part is fast. My fingers are slow. Too much vodka last night. My fingers are usually fast. This morning they are dull. The piccolo player shrieks in my ear. My head hurts. I count the rest bars, and catch the solo entry. I play the rapid quavers. Correct, but loudly. A shadow passes over the music stand. The baton drops.

"Don't you see the big piano over there?"

Captain Janse is screaming. At me. What's the piano got to do with this? I look at the piano, unopened. Then I translate. He means *piano.* Italian musical term for 'softly'. My head clears. Fast.

"From the double bar."

A shadow passes over the music stand once more. Distracting. I turn to the window. The curtains have been stolen. Inspector Malan, the bar manager from the Police Canteen is the size of a piano. He waves his wallet. At me. I owe him R50. Last night's binge. I count the bars until my entry. Eight-and, seven-and, six-and . . .

"Concentrate!" Captain Janse has seen me looking out the window. He can't see Inspector Malan who is running his finger slowly across his throat. Universal sign language every debtor understands. Sweat beads on my upper lip. Two-and breathe in . . .

"Flute!"

I'm a bar early.

"You just don't get it, do you?"

Or a bar too late.

Slam

The mother tried to hug the girl, but she pulled back, shrugging her off. Her daughter was returning after a long time away. The mother would learn how to be a Mom again. Then she would know when to hug, when to stand back.

Fifteen years earlier, the daughter had been a premature infant in an incubator weighing just a kilogram. Then the mother used to drive to the hospital at 4 a.m. to watch her breathe. She'd made up lullabies and slept sitting up beside the monitors. She'd knitted pixie caps for her head the size of an apple, but one morning when she'd been away, a nurse from the adult section deputising in the neo-natal ICU put the wrong tape on the baby's face to secure the feeding tube. When it had to be removed, the outer layer of skin had ripped, leaving a scab and then a scar on the infant's cheekbone that eventually faded to look like a faint silvery fish.

When she was a toddler, the mother had to quit using soap to cure the girl's eczema. She'd slather her in aqueous cream that made a scum on the inside of the tub. The mother fretted about damage from the African sun, begging the girl to wear a hat, to apply sunscreen, warning her about wrinkles and cancer. Later, on the alternate weekends when the daughter was a visitor, she'd ask her mother for medicated creams for pimples, and moisturiser. They'd shop together. The mother would buy her perfume too, saying, Remember me when you smell this.

The girl has new scars like purple slugs in serried ranks, crawling up her arm, but hard to the touch. After she'd slashed herself, the dermatologist offered scar plasters, but the deepest cuts approached the artery. The mother rubs rosehip oil on her child's skin, trying to loosen the keloid tissue, remembering the old worries, airy now as soda bubbles, light as rice paper confetti.

When she was married to her child's father, her own skin was clear. There were never marks from sleep deprivation, no bruises from the interrogations at eleven, at midnight, at one, at two. Only the slow-hitting hours that bore witness to the fear.

Now the mother listens in the quiet hours as her daughter turns in her sleep. She hears the bed springs squeak when the girl gets up for the toilet. In the silence she wonders about matric dance dresses, wedding gowns. The girl draws with pencil crayon in her notebook, sleeves of lace or voile, long skirts to cover the slashes criss-crossing her shins, her thighs.

When the girl has gone to school the mother finds the designs crumpled in the garbage. She takes them out and as she irons them, the air fills with the scent of hot paper.

Fist Mountain

The road to Limpopo is straight and empty on a Sunday morning. The yellow police van rattles through the dusty dry plains of the Bafokeng platinum fields northeast of Pretoria. Our unit, the Police Band, Soweto, is heading to Pholokwane for the annual cultural eisteddfod.

Visible in the far distance are a few huts scattered at the base of a rocky outcrop. Each of my colleagues has a different name for the hill.

"Do you see that mountain?" asks Inspector Dube.

"Mountain?"

"Over there," he jerks his head toward it.

It doesn't look like a mountain. I grew up with real mountains in Cape Town – dangerous ones. Our house overlooks the back of Table Mountain, a natural monument that commands climbers and photographers from around the world. There's Devil's Peak and Skeleton Gorge, where three boys from my school fell to their death on a Boy Scout trip. From the top of our street, the Hottentot's Holland range is visible, snow-capped in winter. A friend's brother died from hypothermia while hiking in a storm.

I point and say, "I see a hill." Dube slaps my hand away.

"What? Why?" I ask, rubbing the finger he walloped.

He raises a fist in front of my face, a sudden and startling gesture. I wonder which taboo I've unwittingly violated this time.

"You must never!" he says, eyes wide and white in his dark face. "We call that place Ntaba Kayikhonjwa. In English it's the Mountain of No Pointing because when you speak its name, your face changes, your body shakes. You must never point that side; only show your fist to indicate direction. Or terrible things happen."

He speaks with theatrical eye-rolling and lip-wobbling. The van erupts laughing. Then I wonder if they're laughing at me because I am a gullible mlungu who has just been told a preposterous story.

Maybe they are laughing because terrifying and mysterious things happen here anyway and are made more bearable with laughter. Children have been found dead, with body parts missing.

"In our culture," says Sergeant Mboweni, "we call it Fist Mountain. You must not stare at that mountain, because if you do, the ancestors will strike you with the fist." He slams a fist into his flattened palm. "Or they hit the one you love."

I am astonished. Again, they laugh.

"You do not believe such a thing?"

"I believe, Sergeant. But how do the villagers avoid gazing upwards? How is it possible?"

"That's not the real story," says Constable Mokwoena, who comes from the region. I can't easily understand his thick accent. "Don't listen the wrong story. The mountain, we call Modimolle. My grandmother told me when I was still young. The ancestors ran from the impis of Shaka, hiding here."

Mokwoena, I note, nods out the back window at the hill receding in the distance, also not pointing. "The mountain protected our people, so the people named mountain Modimolle, which means God's Blessing."

Three days later, returning to Joburg, my colleagues are asleep in the van. As we pass Fist Mountain, I cannot look away. I stare, riveted. I want to know more about this mysterious place. Perhaps I might negotiate a deal with the ancient spirits.

It would help to believe in something now. Merilyn, my mother-in-law, is in hospital in renal failure. She saw fairies when she was a child, and collects miniatures in porcelain and pewter. She plants impatiens in the garden for them. Or used to before she got ill.

I'd been sitting at her bedside, asking her to tell me the story again. She said, "They were swathed in bands of colour. Such pretty colours too: lilac and mauve, yellow and gold."

"How old were you when you saw them, Mum?" I asked.

Her dying has been so painful, so slow. When I'd wiped her lips with a moist flannel, I accidentally rubbed off her skin. Small droplets of blood formed on her lips.

"About five or six. Mary was four."

"What do fairies do?" I ask. Her pale white skin has turned yellow and become bloated.

"They hovered over our heads and waved to us. People have always laughed at me when I talked about it; they think I'm joking."

"But you aren't."

"I saw them," she says, battling to breathe, but smiling.

If I stare at the mountain, perhaps the fairies (who are surely relations of the ancestors) will fetch her. I will them to call her to the other side. If I point at Fist Mountain, the deities might grant a cross-cultural exchange.

The road to Limpopo Province is straight and empty on a Sunday morning. It is three months since the trip with the band, two months since Merilyn's funeral. I drive alone.

I stop next to a wire fence that keeps the cows from wandering onto the road. I walk up the hill to a chain-link fence at the base of the mountain. I remove a china fairy from my bag and place her beside the creosoted post, pointing her serene gaze towards the jagged rock.

The fairy will remind the mountain god of my grateful thanks for opening the hands of the ancestors who took Merilyn home.

Flaw

The elderly Portuguese man selling the house was clean-shaven.
He said he had black thumbs, waggling them for her inspection.
But the discolouration was liver spots and the yellowed patch
between his index and middle finger from cigarettes. He told
a funny story about how everything he tended died. His pit-bull
terrier wagged a stumpy tale in agreement. The woman laughed,
and thought about moving the irises to a shadier spot, dividing
the roots of the agapanthus and clivias that grew too close together.

Beard-like tufts hung from an aloe that grew in a twist against
the shabby perimeter wall. Brown drips wept from Rusty nails
embedded in the concrete panels. Now, when she sees it, she
wonders how she missed the plant's ghoulishness, the sorrowful wall.
At the time, she had merely suspected poor soil. She'd thought about
bright paint.

The old man told another story, laughing, about how the dog had
chased kaffirs out the yard, carrying off a shoe. She winced under
the smile on her face, hating herself for not challenging him,
regretting that she remained silent. She would burn sage, to cleanse
the house of the hate speech.

A black flash of movement through the rockery, like a whipped
shoelace, caught her attention. Snakes, she asked. Lizards, he said.
Later she wondered why she hadn't left then, but the house was a
good price, with lots of space. She hoped her children might return
to her. It was near their school. They were growing up and could
choose for themselves where they wanted to live.

The house had big windows and the sun streamed through in all
seasons. Loeries and coucals flitted through the garden. A pair
of hadedahs swooped onto the pool fence each evening, then hopped
down to the water's edge to drink.

The seller laughed a lot. He had worked as a lighting engineer
and rigged neon lights that flickered on when the power failed.

71

He'd placed hidden speakers in the pelmets so that music played in every room of the house, even the bathrooms. Surround sound, he said, the gold cap on his tooth glinting, the tatty velvet carpet uneven under foot.

She was thrilled when the sale went through. Doubly thrilled when her daughter said she wanted to move in. The woman would learn to be a mother again, she'd drive her girl to school in the mornings, go watch her sports events in the afternoons.

Before the furniture arrived, they slept all four of them on borrowed mattresses on the shabby velvet carpet in the lounge. It was a cold July but the night sky was clear. She lay awake watching the stars setting, looking at the tail of the Southern Cross, remembered where she'd come from, glad to have survived.

The movers shuttled back and forth from the truck to the front door. She directed them around the house. Bookshelves here, antique dresser there.

When the contractors came to lay new carpets, they discovered slasto underneath. Purply-brown sheets of slate made a crazy patchwork. She fingered the glue balls stuck to the stone and asked if it would clean up nicely. She imagined a rustic finish, like she'd seen in game park rondavels. It would compliment the wooden ceiling. She liked natural textures.

Slasto is a menace, said the carpet guy. It chips and bubbles. It flakes of in chunks. Even if you seal it.

The new carpet would never be level unless she pulled up the slasto and threw a new screed. He warned about the mess: We have to take picks to it, rip up the old screed. She looked at the piano, wondered where she'd put it while workmen pounded through the house.

She asked about other options. Lay extra under-felt so that you feel the variation less. She imagined walking, as if on a mattress. Anything else? Live with it, said the contractor.

Mango Chutney

"What can you see up there, Antjie?"

"Hessian sacks, old newspapers, sixty years of dust."

"What's hessian, Auntie Grieta?"

"Antjie, what's hessian in American?"

"Burlap. Hey, Grieta, hold the ladder still."

"Got it!"

"Jeez. Didn't Ouma keep a maid?"

"Yes. Her name was Precious. Ouma grumbled a lot about her. She always said she did precious little."

"Evidently. This place is filthy. Here, take this box."

"Got it."

"Careful, it's heavy."

"Mind, Katrien. You're in the way."

"What else is up there?"

"Dead toasters, broken light fittings, worthless crap."

"We'll have to turf it all out."

"Why, Auntie?"

"Because Ouma was a zealous hoarder, I'm a Zen Buddhist and you're not taking junk back to Connecticut!"

"Wow, you two, check this old newspaper out! 'Verwoerd – A Nation Mourns.' September 7, 1966."

"I doubt Precious's family mourned too hard for him."

"Who was he, Auntie Griet? Was he important?"

"You could say so. They made a play about the guy who killed him."

"That crazy Greek?"

"Yes. I saw the show at The Baxter. His name was Tsafendas. His mother was the family's maid."

"Sheesh! You have to keep your eyes on the servants."

"In America we've an au pair. Her name's Frieda, from Norway. She likes the boat and Dad says she's luscious and . . ."

"Katrien! Enough."

"Why Mom?"

"Let's just say, 'We had an au pair', okay?"

"Has Frieda gone, Mom?"

"I refuse to discuss this."

"Hey, Katrien, what's in that box?"

"Jam, Auntie."

"That jam is mango chutney. The label shows February 1975."

"What's chutney?"

"A South African tradition. You eat it with curry."

"Ouma made it with sugar, vinegar, spices and fruit. Usually mango, but sometimes apples or apricots."

"Can I taste it?"

"Ja, it's good."

"I wouldn't."

"Relax, Antjie, it won't hurt. She might as well have a taste of her heritage."

"Relax? I'm not rushing her to hospital at midnight with food poisoning. Just throw the whole damn lot out. Can't she just leave the 'African Experience' alone this once?"

"Hey. It's preserved, Antjie. Sugar doesn't go off."

"You'll be driving her to the emergency room, got that?"

"Relax, Mom. Frieda says Mom's very uptight."

"Shut up, Katrien. Shut the hell up."

"Let's taste it together. We'll share a hospital ward if we get sick."

"It won't open, Auntie."

"Don't even try, Kiddo. It's off. Pitch it in the garbage."

"Ouma sealed it perfectly. Let me help. It's just a wax disk. To keep it fresh."

"Fresh after 30 years?"

"I want a taste. We're going to try some, aren't we, Katrien?"

"Neat! But there's something in it, Auntie Griet."

"Ag no. Perhaps you'd better turf it after all."

"Auntie, is putting money in food another African tradition?"

"No . . ."

"There's something in here, like a silver dollar . . . but gold."

"A Kruger Rand!"

"Look, Auntie, the man's nose is covered by a raisin."

"Ouma never trusted the servants."

"At least she trusted them not to steal her husband."

Purification

My blood is hot and my skin too tight. No choir in the empty chapel but sirens like razor blades. The supplicants left only yesterday's prayers. Even the old monk has gone. My favourite children's book showed how whole blood was processed, a rotor separating the plasma from red cells. I read it until it fell apart and my father stuck it back together with wide clear tape. I turn a slow circle on the rust and bone coloured floor, wooden tiles like we had in my childhood home. I see altar and cross, window and pew, remember how I lingered over pictures of platelets, that looked like dishes clamouring along pencil-sketch veins. I held my hands to the bedside lamp, marvelling at the pink light that shone through my fingers. I circle again, gathering momentum. The mosaic tiles blur and blend. A game, twirling on the lush grass. We fell, laughing, my sisters and me in matching candy-striped dresses. When the clouds stopped swirling and the trees quit bobbing, we got up, did it again. But this autistic whizzing keeps my feet turning, past the altar-cross-window-pew, even as my head says, Stop, my arms fly up, level with my shoulders. A fan in my parent's room groaned and thumped. I'd switch it on to watch the blades speed up, merge into one, then switch it off and nod to the rhythmic deceleration. My feet won't stop. The rotation accelerates: altarcrosswindowpewaltar. If I fall, my head will split like a melon. My father drew diagrams on the back of an envelope, explained optical illusions, warned how a fan's blade would cut off fingers, but an invisible aeroplane rotor could chop off your head. I slip, bang my shoulder, grasp at the plaster, slump against a pew. The scene is a zoetrope, the altar and unlit candles twitch and flicker. On a roundabout with peeling green paint I spun the girls until they screamed. I tried to stop it; my arm ripped hard in the socket, flung me in a trajectory, legs kicking wild. My sisters weaved and giggled, sinking down on soft leaves.

Eavesdropping

Nel is already in bed, naked, typing on her laptop. It's nearly midnight and still too hot for pyjamas. The overhead fan has loosened a ceiling board and the adjoining strip bumps and separates with each rotation. It sounds like Christmas beetles singing.

Jaap talks to himself in the bathroom. Nel, who is listening to a jazzy arrangement of 'Between the Devil and the Deep Blue Sea', turns down the music.

She hopes he's grumbling about the church and not her. He doesn't talk much, so when he does, she wants to know what's being said. It seems the priest has increased his duties and Jaap no longer wants to play piano at the family service.

He'll tell her when he's discussed it with himself. Jaap is an organist who studied Bach and Handel, Tallis and Vivaldi. He loves the formal harmonies and the intricate counterpoint of the ancients. He doesn't mind the genteel ceremony of the early Mass that the pensioners attend. But the church organ is a wreck, needing repairs. Sometimes as the lowest notes vibrate the ceiling, bits of plaster crumble and fall on his head. That really annoys him. She hears about it through the bathroom door on Sunday mornings after church as he combs the plaster flakes out his greying wisps.

Jaap has many piano pupils at the school nearby, so he's too busy to practise the organ regularly, which is probably just as well because the low pedal notes stick, driving him berserk. The priest doesn't want to spend money on fixing it. The organ is old fashioned. He believes that what they really need is a digital system, a multi-media interactive computerised set up. It sets Jaap's teeth on edge. The priest wants marimbas. The church needs transformation in the new South Africa.

Through the bathroom door, Nel hears Jaap complain, "Not enough chunka-chunka guitars, every damn one of them untuned? Not enough glory-bloody-hallelujah to last a thousand life times? Get marimbas, why don't you? Let's go native. Split my head open with a machete."

When he turns on the shower, to wash the remnants of his haircut that have prickled his neck all day, she can no longer hear the specifics, only him railing at the pale green tiles in the cubicle, yelling what he'd like to tell the priest. She knows better than to interrupt.

When he emerges in checked pyjamas, his hair a moist fuzz, she says, "Won't you bring me another glass of water?"

His eyes flare. He blinks, looking at her as if he's never seen her before. "The glass," she says, "please fill it."

"The glass?" he says.

"Over there. I left it on the bookshelf."

"Of course." Jaap fills it and sets it down beside her, then rests his hand on her head as if delivering a blessing.

He climbs into bed and opens a hymn book, studying the chords, analysing the cadences. As he counts the syllables of 'Praise the Saviour' his lips move silently. Nel flips her laptop closed and says, "What are you reading tonight?" She knows the answer. It's always the same hymnal. But it's a trick question. He doesn't tell her about the six-four progressions, the five-seven resolutions, the suspended minors. He'll tell her, as she strokes his head, about the composer. Jaap knows the oddest things.

"This one's by an Irishman, Thomas Kelly, who wrote 765 hymns in his life time. He left the Irish church and became a Dissenter. He was a good man who was remembered for his acts of generosity during the Irish potato famine of 1847."

Nel, who would like a little act of generosity, says, "My good man, can I help you repair your organ?"

Parrot Syllabus

"Hello, Beaks."

That's how my mother greets the birds as she enters. Her basket contains carrots, leeks and potatoes pulled from the garden. Rhubarb too. She's planned syllabub for tonight's pudding. The bird cages are lined up on the back veranda by the kitchen door; seed husks litter the red concrete floor.

Mum can never remember the animals' names. She calls all nine dogs Paws and all seven cats Claws. I say, "This is Jemima, Mum, and she's a Senegal Parrot." Jemima's on my shoulder preening her emerald feathers, acting angelic. She bows her head, the signal that I may scratch her neck.

Mum leans in close. "You going to crap on my carpet, Beak?"

Jemima doesn't like that. Quick as a mamba, she bites Mum's eyebrow, hanging on as her scaly claws scrabble for purchase against Mum's cheek.

"Get this fucking beak off me!" screams Mum, batting at the flapping wings. I can't. I'm laughing too hard. Jemima flutters to the floor, scowling. "Fuck," says Mum again, rubbing her eyebrow. "That was fucking sore." I try to say, Don't swear, Mum, but Jemima is mimicking my laughter and tears stream down my face.

"Tomorrow Jemima's going to echo *that* new word," I say.

"Tomorrow Jemima's going to be parrot soup," says Mum.

Sawubona Mfowethu!

There is an empty tub of lemon balm lip-gloss in my bag, a nearly finished disposable lighter that I can't throw out because I am still grieving the loss of my cigarettes. Also, four mashed tissues filled with snorted tears I cried all over Calvinia's couch all over yesterday.

The remittance advice for my registration for "Learn to Speak Zulu" is crumpled now. Should I throw it out or keep it for my tax return? Perhaps this time I will progress beyond the rudiments of 'Sawubona, Mfowethu!' Greetings, my brother!

Samuel Sandwick's business card with fancy fonts has curled at the corners. He's the estate agent who asked about taking music lessons at our neighbour's show day, he was very eager, but I got the sense he doesn't want to play scales and arpeggios as much as he wants to ball my husband, the classical guitar teacher. That, or he wants a sole mandate to sell our house on Busy Street.

Directions scribbled on the back of an envelope were to Regina Mundi Cathedral in Soweto where I held a candle at the memorial service for AIDS orphans. While the chaplain read, "Suffer little children to come unto me," I wept for my recurrent miscarriages, for the sleepless nights and painful injections, the expensive infertility treatments that inevitably end in livery chunks flushed down the toilet.

A pamphlet with the nutritional facts of all McDonalds' food items reveals that I gobbled down 1,833.93 kJ with the Super Size Fries right after my last visit to the dietician. I shouldn't have ordered the McFlurry with Oreos.

Government free-issue condoms. I paid five bucks to a traffic light beggar for those. Clever bugger. Suppurating boils covered his face. He grinned when I said, "Sawubona," but the boil in the corner of his mouth oozed. I dropped the change from Ronald McDonald gingerly into his hand, but couldn't figure how to say in Zulu that I want neither a man nor condoms. I guessed at where else his boils oozed, regretted my lack of thought control, then heaved the fries into the garbage as soon as I stopped.

I picked up a leaflet for a miracle-working craniosacral therapist at the manicurist after my French nail add-ons had set: *Jubilate's gentle hands-on technique assures a deep-healing process whereby every cell in the body expresses a rhythmic movement which is fundamental to life, curing multiple deep-seated traumas . . .*

This I will keep. I will not it throw away. For surely now, I will get pregnant, Calvinia will be out of a job, world peace is imminent, and HIV/AIDS will be a distant blimp on yesterday's horizon?

Jubilate Deo!

Oprah's Girl

"Poplap," said my mom patting the couch next to her, one sober morning before my birthday. Ouma's present had arrived early and I sat on the floor watching Oprah, while I dressed my 'First Love' in the hat and booties of the same hideous mauve that Ouma had used to knit my birthday jersey.

"Lilac," I'd said to Ouma, "lilac is the *in* colour."

I smiled anyway and said, "Thanks, Ouma, that's terrible nice." I wished I was Oprah's girl.

"Poplap," said my mom, prodding me in the backside with her bony toes, "you're eleven tomorrow and you're going to be a woman soon. Things happen when the moon shines full."

I nodded, wondering if she wanted me to fetch her something, a ciggie or nail polish.

"You can still play with your dolls, just look after your virginity. You can't buy another if you lose it." That day she bought me tampons wrapped in shocking pink plastic for my birthday present. One fell from my purse at the movies and rolled under the seat. It looked like a giant sweet, too big for sucking.

When I complained, she told me about the pads she'd used at my age, as fat and lumpy as rolled socks that looped into a gauze belt which was visible above the waistband of your skirt if your blouse was too short. When Ouma was a girl, she'd sewn her own cloth lappies that hung on the wash line for all to see. "Count yourself lucky," she said.

But I cried and cried in the toilet at school because even though I pushed and twisted, I couldn't get the tampon in. So Desiree told Meisie who told Mieta who told Miss van der Molen, who passed me a neat little package under the door. It folded open with wings and glue strips that stuck to my pantie and my pubes, but I didn't complain.

Terror Hot

My best friend Faridah tells me she's moving to Terror Hot, her husband's hometown in Indiana.

"Don't you mean Terre Haute?" I say.

"It's what I said," she says.

"It sounds bad the way you said it."

"It's a dangerous place. They do not love Muslims in America."

I am in the hospital. The doctor shows me to the ward.

Faridah a non-conformist, refuses to wear a burkah, but she doesn't want to leave Pretoria, doesn't want to leave home.

"Why did you marry an American then?" I ask. Faridah is sweet, but stupid.

I was her bridesmaid, in a gown of lilac chiffon at a Western-style wedding. Brad is a bear. He worships Faridah but never goes to Mosque.

I believe a cyst has made my belly round, but the doctor says I'm pregnant.

Brad makes a fortune as an importer. We whisper about him, wondering what precisely he imports. Amarah reckons he's a drug lord. Naaila says he's just a charmer selling fake Nikes to the Nigerians. I figure he makes porn vids, or at least that's what I tell the girls.

My uncle has come to stay in the ward. He makes it sound like he's there to look after me, but he's really come to watch me. There are lots of visitors. I want them all to leave, but they stay, making small talk. They think this is a party. I don't want my uncle to stay in the ward, we are not close. He is not one to be trusted.

"Don't worry, Faridah, you don't look Muslim," I say.

"You and Brad will make pretty babies, maybe with blue eyes," says Naaila. Faridah is light-skinned and blue-eyed. Brad has red hair and a ruddy complexion.

I tell the nurse I don't want a Caesarean, but the doctor says

I must. I want to deliver naturally. I don't want to be cut.

"Do they get hurricanes in Terror Hot?" asks Faridah. Brad says, "Just a tornado now and then. An occasional cyclone. Snow. Lots of snow."

I want to leave the ward, to walk about the hospital. I dismantle a mirror in the bathroom wall – the way out. My visitors talk loudly and don't hear me unscrewing the glass, which is actually a screen on wheels that jiggles and clanks as I move it. They don't notice I've gone.

We gather for a last supper together at the Spur near the airport. The cauliflower mush is lukewarm, the steak is stringy. Brad says, "You get the best meat in the US, just the best."

I walk through the hospital, recognising it, remembering.
I'm waiting for the new moon.

"It's a great place to raise kids," says Brad. Faridah sits straighter, looks more determined. I pick the sunflower seeds out the bread that crumbles when I butter it.

The hospital is where I spent some months recovering after the attack in the Baha'i Centre, after my divorce, after getting kicked out of the community because I was living with my lover.

Faridah's mother cries at OR Tambo International. It's February and humid. "Stop the brouhaha, Mama," Faridah says. I say, "Don't worry, Mrs Osman. She'll be back soon. Our Faridah doesn't like the cold." Her father plucks his beard and beseeches her to reconsider. Brad doesn't even look remorseful.

But this hospital is not a regular hospital with a maternity ward.
The plane is delayed because of an electric storm.

This hospital is the psychiatric institution where I once shared the ward with an Arabian princess who claimed to have been rescued by a prince on a fine horse. When the woman in the bed across from us took off her clothes and showed us her cunt, I said, "Where is your prince now?" The ward always smelled of piss because the cunt woman refused to use the toilet. She said she was waiting for the second coming, she couldn't sit down.

Faridah looks scared.

So why am I back here, pregnant, needing somewhere to deliver my baby? I return to the ward, climb back through the mirror.
The party is over, the nurse has cleaned up. My uncle is gone and I say to the nurse, "Help me."

Secretly, I think Brad is an al-Qaeda operative.

I'm ready to deliver. Please keep the doctor away. Don't let him cut me. Just give me time, please, give me time.

Prometheus's Child

My autistic son won't say his name.

"Why not?" says his father, pouring another brandy. "How hard can that be? He's four years old, Godammit!"

Jim folds small squares of paper into eagles, dinosaurs and multi-pointed stars. Sometimes he tries to set the house alight.

When the shopping list, electricity bill, pharmacy statement, and the cash I left on the fridge to buy groceries disappear, I search my desk, my briefcase, the hallstand. I head to the shops, trying to remember what was on the list: cheese, fennel, bread – glad of my credit card.

When I tuck Jim up I discover the missing items in his bedroom, transformed to inhabit a more luminous world. With regret I retrieve them from that shimmering place, unfolding the angels and owls with heavy hands, sending them back as pedestrian signals on my dull path.

I wish Jim's origami dragon would breathe on the monstrous therapy bill and burn up the overdraft, instead of igniting flash points of another migraine.

I wish Jim's father would go easy on the gin, on the jibes. It's that which pecks away my liver today.

Diner

Halfway through a wilted radish that burns my tongue and withers my resolve, the penny drops through the slot of the divine fantabular. Picky eaters all over the diner regain their senses, call for management and complain about the troops of mediocrity blooming on every spoon.

Halfway through a conversation with Mr Grunt, I see under a lettuce frond the floor of my heart, replicated in the patterned leaf, a bind and grump, bump and grind, and when that mediocre management comes calling, they ask about my yearning for yams. There is no Yum, no mum, no maybe no more. No oh ho? No ho ho, no yes please, no no. So?

Halfway home through the eve of my fortieth, lust gusts up through my ovaries, whistling woohoo and yeehi and whyevernot? So I dial Mr Yum and call up Miss Knot. They swing me from the ceiling tree, manage my fetish, backsided, backslided, praying and pricking. No bump, but a bang, no grind but a gang, they floor me and thaw me, they more and more me.

Halfway through the fight of the night, Mr Grim, Mr Gaunt, Mr Glum all take flight. Bring your carrots and cucumbers, your beans and your marrow. Drop your pennies, drop my panties, under-rod your jockeys, boys. They say, Salad days are over; we've another restaurant to run, so eat out or suck up, swallow or spit; get a fresh dish for loopy fruit, and do remember to pop your pills.

Halfway to bed through a post-party sigh I say, Stay Mr Yum. Don't go yet Miss Knot. It's that fired up the tired time with my backside roped tender, radishes showing, cherry still glowing. Rise up for the feast, squeeze the orange, turf dead ducks. I say, Spoon me, don't spleen me, it's time for the fill up, no foul up, nor fuck up, just eat me and please me, knead me, please need me.

Mrs Popcorn

She is round and kind and her skin is white, and her stomach rolls and neck rolls and great hanging arms make you think of popcorn. Her hair too, which is tight blonde curls. Her real surname is Greek and unpronounceable, but she's not Greek, only married to one.

When it's hot, she jumps in the school pool, dress and all, cooling off in the water, then she flops onto the hot concrete and steams in the sun to warm up again. When the children push and shove to get their sandwiches and pies, she says in a Brakpan accent, "This is not a race. Everyone's a winner. Nobody go hungry by Popcorn's Paleis." Sometimes she slips me a lollypop for free and says, "You can have it, it's kosher." To the Muslim children she says, "Salaam, Sonny" and "Inshallah, Baby".

On the day that I am standing first in line, Mrs Popcorn tramps through a glob of mayonnaise spilled on the tiles. Her foot skids out and her ankle snaps. There, right in front of me, while I'm drowning my soggy chips in tomato sauce.

Her bone pokes out her skin, the same colour as my chips, blood like tomato sauce, only it doesn't squeeze out in a gentle leak. It gushes. The children stop pushing and shoving. For once it is silent outside the tuck shop. When the ambulance men come, they try and try, but they cannot lift the stretcher with her on it. We watch from afar, crying. Mrs Popcorn is going to die.

Duet

When the man put his gun to my head, I heard a click. Not the click of the trigger. I never heard that. Even if I had I would not be here to recount it. A switch tripped in my skull, below my eyebrows, above my nose. The gunman's finger played with the safety catch of his glock: flick-flick-flicking, like playing with a ballpoint. I wanted to tell him to stop but he was in no mood to be ordered about.

I couldn't stop talking after that. I chattered without pausing. Dirty words accumulated on the chinaware, conflict lingered in the coffee cups. Night after day, I washed them clean of wicked gossip, swear words and secrets. Day after night, they dirtied again with more of the same until someone took me to hospital.

In the ward was a man who couldn't talk.

I asked the cleaner why. He swished his broom, making me jump. I asked the nurse. She rattled a pill bottle at me. The doctor said it was none of my business and asked if I fed my meds to the pot plants.

Outside, the oaks dropped leaves on my head.

One patient told me his ex-wife had used a carving knife to slit his throat. A second said he had paid a doctor to excise his speech organs. A third said he had swallowed ground glass and lye.

"Beckfluto, blokfluit," hissed a coffee urn in the lounge.

When tolerably satisfied with life, the man who couldn't speak took a plastic recorder from the music therapy room. He took a slow deep breath, placed his fingers over the holes, and blew a stream of air through the mouthpiece, emitting twittery chirrups. He'd watch the stream meandering through the hospital grounds, stared at the mossy ferns, trilling, warbling. The sound was crimson shards when he was angry, an iron-grey keening when sad.

The silent man me preached in his sleep that night: unfathomable warnings, promises of archangels, and tales of abandoned cherubs.

His speech loss was surely reversible.

Next morning, everyone had something to say. "He grunts," said a lady knitting a baboon.

"He babbles," said a boy who knotted together stolen chairs.

"He gurgles," said an uncle wearing disposable pants.

"Blokflojte, blockflöte," squeaked a linen basket on castors.

I took out my own recorder – the rosewood Dolmetsch – from the bedside table and started to blow. We tried a recorder duet, a call-and-response recitative that nobody understood.

"Blockflöjt, blockflötték," murmured the medicine cabinet's padlocks.

The patients looked up, momentarily transfigured by the duet we blew: love songs from the movies and oratorios before handover, *Jesus Loves Me* while the staff exchanged patient reports. I wanted to ask about Jesus but my voice was gone. A twelve-tone serial pattern flew out of my instrument instead, a jarring seven-beat rhythm: SCHOEN-berg PEN-de-rec-ki BERG . . .

As suddenly as we started we stopped. The humid anguish in the ward could not bear our effort. Patients in fetal positions exhaling steam clouds had waterlogged our instruments.

That night we held hands across the aisle between our lumpy cots. Next morning, a flock of guinea fowl eclipsed the sun and hovered about the ward.

I woke to find "Blockflauta," tattooed on my arm, and "Blockfleita," on his. Everywhere was blood. Under the bed, in sharp splinters lay his recorder, or perhaps what I saw were sticks, or the spines of autumn leaves that blew in through the window. It wasn't clear through the cloud of guinea fowl feathers and the screaming of my duet partner. He struggled against two orderlies who were also smeared in blood – or so I thought until a nurse aide scrubbed the red painted lettering off my arm under the bathroom tap. She cursed the fool who left the art cupboard unlocked.

"He jumped on his recorder to make it work again," explained the lady stitching a bassoon.

"He carved a heart on your arm while you slept," said the boy, blowing soap bubbles through a spool.

"He anointed you," said the auntie weaving a daisy chain.

The staff, which disliked his wailing pipe and mess in general,
put him in the cry room without his recorder. The cry room is not
like the partitioned space at church where babies are breastfed.
Covered mattresses are riveted to the floor and bolsters line the walls.

"Why have they taken him away?" I asked the janitor who chased
me with his broom. I asked the nurse to take him my recorder.
She gave me another pill. I asked the doctor if there were visiting
hours in the cry room, but he prescribed a sleep-deprived EEG
for me.

I watched from the cry room window. Colour faded from his
cheeks. When he was as grey as the stuffing that wept from the walls,
he lay down to die. I took my recorder out of my pocket and played
to him, *Nearer my God to Thee.*

That night by lamplight from the nurse's station, a ceramic plate,
spinning like a flying saucer, hovered above his bed, an art therapy
project. Painted with shaky strokes of a fine bristled brush were the
words: silence is golden. I caught the spinning plate and replaced
it on the wall.

I awoke next day under my bed. The medics were discussing my
EEG. The first doctor asked if the recorder was an instrument of
music. The second answered: an instrument of torture.
The professor, said, "Stop her Fluanxol. Wean the Lithium.
Halve the Prozac. This is straightforward post-traumatic stress.
Why kill a mosquito with a glock?"

"Blockflauta, blockfleita!" agreed a kiln from the occupational
therapy workshop.

I could finally be still if my duet partner would say his name.
If we break the plate the speech vault will open. We'll leave together.
But if it's a flying saucer in disguise, we'll never go

I rub the spot below my eyebrows, above my nose, waiting for the
switch to turn on his voice, turn off mine.

Naysayers

Our relatives fly back from Melbourne and Sydney and Perth at Christmas to Johannesburg, and note on the road from the airport how even more beggars scour the landfill dump than there were before. They sneer at hawkers at intersections, comment on the razor wire atop our wall. They brag about their picket fences and clean streets, their ordered traffic. We reassure them that life is not so bad, that some fancy London designer is ordering loads of African beadwork for her High Street fashion boutique, that Manchester United is going to visit next year and *Tsotsi* just won an Oscar. Things are getting better, we have Broadband now. We can Skype around the world for less than the cost of a McDonalds burger. But we have to agree that no, we don't walk in the streets, and yes, rolling blackouts suck and the water gets turned off every now and again (and again) and yes, our Vice-President raped a young woman with HIV and got off scot-free, and sure it's open season on our women now. We don't love our country so much when the Aussies are here, but our farewell embraces three weeks later leave us feeling better. Driving home from the airport with our boots empty, our guest rooms clear again, we feel freer, somehow.

Promise

Anita's little sister wears a lime green fleecy tracksuit with a cross-eyed hedgehog on the front. It is too big for her, a hand-me-down Anita refused to wear. Lime green was never her colour, but the fabric was a terrific bargain.

It is the only item their mother ever made on the sewing machine – a 'Sprinter' with 63 decorative stitches. Even more fancy stitches came with the computer card that slotted in behind the thread spool for just another 49 bucks. The stitches worked perfectly on the television, but as soon as Anita's mother tried it at home, they tangled in the bobbin case and the needle broke.

When she tried again, the fabric crinkled under the presser foot. She unpicked it, but the fabric was punctured with holes, so she appliquéd the hedgehog over the whole irksome fiasco. She sewed on buttons for eyes instead of satin stitch embroidery and glued on a patch of felt for the muzzle.

The sewing machine migrated like a pterodactyl to the basement where it roosts now beside the bread baker that also worked only once, the ice-cream maker that made frozen slush tasting of raw egg, the knitting machine that made knotty scarves and the step walker that was supposed to give you firm buttocks and thin thighs.

Anita dreams of a dinosaur that watches television in a clearing where round-bellied women wear loincloths and bake bread on flat rocks beside an open fire. Under layers of ancient earth they discover fossilised remains of inkjet re-fill kits and hand-held vacuum cleaners.

Next morning her mother is on the phone, ordering a silicone bra to enhance her bosom so she can wear evening gowns without plucking at the straps. Anita's mother has no evening gowns.

A Hundred Times a Day

I look down the road a hundred times a day, like a nervous tic, searching for you, a sighting, watching for dust, waiting for the angel trumpets that will herald your return. I listen every moment.
I will not put on the radio or television because I am feeling for your footsteps. In the garden, I dig and plant, but between thrusts of the spade in the earth, around the sound of water spraying from the hose, I'm trying to hear an engine, a car, a plane, a sign. There is no telephone here, no cellphone reception, no computer hum making it harder to hear you arrive.

I've studied abandonment in its minutest details for two months, or is it ten years? I am an expert on its unfurling tendrils, hope watered by watching, nurtured by waiting. I am the bachelor, the honours, the master spinster, she-doctor of desertion, professor of the parting ways. My thesis the improbable yearning that does not die hard or fast, my antithesis births slowly like disbelief.

And even after I have uprooted my nostalgia and trampled it with the tawdry halos, even after my hunger-thirst-ache is scorched in the sun, even after it has become brittle as bird bones, alone and splintery, I still look down the road a hundred times a day.

Overdose

When Mr Niehaus accuses us of cheating on the biology test because we both get perfect scores, we deny it. I say, "We can't help being naturally brilliant." Jane says, "But we sit at opposite ends of the class. How could we?" We babble at the same time: "We aren't cheaters. We did nothing wrong. That's so gay."

We both get suspended. That night I text her:

- *dont tell em what we did*
- *i wont. u kiddin?*
- *dont wus out on me now*
- *who u calling wus?*
- *does kylie know?*
- *not frm me. r u scared?*
- *nevah*

Driving to meet the headmaster next day, Dad says, "You've got some please-explaining to do in there. You want to tell me what actually happened, before we go in?" I stare at his pineapple yellow shirt and shake my head. My mother, sedate but sour, says, "We can't help if you won't tell us your version of the story." I say, breathing deeply, "There's nothing to tell." I roll my eyes, but Dad sees me in his rear-view mirror and chides me for insolence.

Jane and I were at Mr Niehaus's house on the weekend, while Jane's older sister, Kylie, was supposed to be babysitting his year-old twins. He'd gone to visit his crazy wife in hospital. We sub-contracted for Kylie so she could bone her boyfriend, Zorro, without her mother knowing what a tart she is.

Mr Niehaus's brats are Penny and Lenny, identical turtles with fat beaky faces and short necks. While they drooled on their stacking bricks, we switched on Mr Niehaus's computer, read his emails, checked the websites stored in his recent history, guessing we'd find porn, but Toughlove.org wasn't about BDSM. We checked out Tearsandhealing.com and CoDependentNoMore.co.za, but it was

95

more boring crap.

Kylie relieved us a half-hour before Mr Niehaus was due to return and split her wages with us later.

"What were you thinking?" says my mother on the way home. Her lemon blouse and golden hair match my father's shirt. Penny and Lenny wore yellow that day too, the colour of the sludge in their nappies.

We were thinking Mr Niehaus is an idiot for giving his kids such dumb names. We were thinking of biology experiments: making the twins strawberry smoothies with a fleck of mustard turd dropped into the blender, or posting a can of tuna through the sound hole of Mr Niehaus's guitar all coated in dust, of mailing his wife our panties. We were thinking how easily we could be really evil, how virtuous we were to resist. We were thinking we were saints because all we did was copy out the questions on the three domains of life: archaea, eukarya and bacteria.

Juicy Lucy's Salvation

Juicy Lucy is bored. She thinks I'm just another pretty boy. Her sneer makes it clear that she doesn't know who I am.

The pretty boys arrive each week, needing cash, every month, blind to her scorn, willing to service titillation where they find it wanting, wanton: elite bachelorette parties in Salvation's northern suburbs, or queer uncles needing friction. They're not fussy. They're needy too, will spread their cheeks when supplies for their nasal recreation run out. They'll get it up to re-inflate their expensive habits. They need money for speed. They need quick money.

The proprietress looks at my résumé. Her disinterest discloses that she doesn't recognise me. She doesn't care for these needy, greedy men. No, Juicy Lucy has other tastes.

They're easy-come-easy-go, the pretty boys, and she thinks I'm just another flitting through her establishment for a month or three. She reads me the rules: "Don't do drugs. Mind your personal hygiene, no body odour or bad breath – got that? Don't bring your partner here. Don't brag about your tips. Don't treat the customers with contempt. Don't slag off other dancers. No fighting. No free dances. Don't shag the other staff."

They're easy to get rid of, the pretty boys. They can't stick to the rules. And Juicy Lucy takes no shit – no, sir. She'll call the cops just as soon as one gets uppity with a customer, or forgets to brush his teeth.

Juicy Lucy is waiting. For me. I promised to arrive unannounced. She waits for a sign – to hear her own name, and the instruction she yearns for – from the one who makes her blood run cold, her cunt run hot, the one for whom she dances on the webcam, the one who says, "Stop right there, Julie-Lou." She is longing to meet the one before whom she drops her eyes, the one to whom she says, "Yes, Master."

"So, what can you do, Mister?" she asks. "You brought a tape, a CD? Got a dance routine?" She squints at my résumé again,

"Where'd you say you worked before?"

Juicy Lucy waits for the sign – the words she knows, her name, my voice – so she can yield to the man before whom she kneels, obedience clamped on her nipples with clothes pegs, slivers of ginger burning her anus. She's waiting for one whose voice soothes her from her computer's speakers, "A bit more pain, for Master, little slave." She is waiting for the one who makes her beg, "Please Master, can your slave come now?" She wants the one who takes her to the brink of her orgasm, and says, "Stop right there, Julie-Lou."

"So, what can you do, Mister?" asks Juicy Lucy, irritated at my silence.

Juicy Lucy waits for the one who hears her frustrated howls, and says, "Stop right there, Julie-Lou. You've pleased me, slave. Now touch yourself, and come."

"So – what can you do, Mister?" she repeats again, reaching for the cigarettes in her breast pocket.

I put my hand over hers, and before she can pull away in surprise, I say, "Stop right there, Julie-Lou."

In the Biscuits

Discord speaks in the insect air. Sometimes it's the computer
buzz, or cables in a snarl beside my bed that make my heart race,
my palms sweat. The modem, the ear phones, the camera toys.
If they were snakes I would not be so fearful. I would chase them
out, saying Shoo! Shoo! Out boys. Other times it's the weevils in
the cupboard, weaving stringy tangles in the biscuits, the flour, the
oats, that make my knees buckle in a faint, because once you've
got weevils you can never get rid of them, unless you buy those
super duper snappy Tuppers, which we can't afford. And I can't be
throwing the flour out every time the webs appear. I can't bear waste,
so I sieve the flour and throw out the tangles, making sure you're not
in the room when I'm picking the weevils out your pancake, turning
the pan on high to kill any eggs. Or it can be the unopened post –
a stack now of bills I'm afraid to open. Debt, like marriage,
a union of being fucked deeper and deeper. After the fanfare, no
more ceremony, just shopping for gear, accumulating kit. Stuff and
things. Too many things.

Christmas Eve Picnic, Pretoria

Under leafy jacaranda branches in our private garden, I wipe down the slatted picnic table I made for you last Christmas. I throw the embroidered cloth you stitched for me over it and set two earthenware dishes on each side.

You place a round of Brie, pale as your breast, beside a salad of herbs, oven-baked bread, olives and pretty slivers of cold ham. I bring a sumptuous fruit bowl with summer jewels of the Cape: hanepoot grapes, fat as your nipple, fuzzy peaches, beautiful as your buttocks, watermelon, litchis, plums.

I wipe crumbs from your mouth after you've eaten, and we clear the table. I undo your ribbon ties, finger your buttons. Your foot on the bench reveals you naked under your skirt. Your hairless flesh is pink as cherry blossoms, inner lips burgundy as the leaves on the prunus. Sandals off, you slip a toe under my shorts. You suck my finger. I run it slowly along your teeth.

My tongue in your ear, I say, "I want you where I want you."

"Eat me," you say.

"Greedy girl! You must wait." I place a gift on the table, telling you to open it.

Tomorrow I will carve a steaming turkey for your family; you will redden as you whip up the brandy butter my mother always praises. Your father will tell us how much he appreciates a traditional dinner. We will all know that what he would really like is a traditional wedding for his only daughter, but we'll let it pass because it's Christmas and the new South Africa and same sex marriages are now constitutional.

My brother will look at your cleavage when he says, "Delicious!" and I will give him a look that says, "Don't even think it!"

Your uncle will stare at my low-slung jeans and say, "You girls, um, ladies, sure cook up a storm, don't you?" We will all laugh at the double entendre and you will shift gingerly in your chair.

You will giggle over the Christmas pudding we both detest, remembering how I tied you to this sturdy table, how I sliced this mango above your belly. Your panties will moisten again recalling how I dribbled juice from the knife blade down your cleft. You will blush to think of me licking this knife before tracing its point around your nipples – a preparatory gesture.

Tomorrow you will be glad that I'm giving you your Christmas present now, and not in front of our families. In a moment you will beg for the gag so the neighbours don't hear because I'm going to test it out, now, under the jacaranda trees: a heavy flogger made of old copper leather – the one you pointed out in the catalogue. I will refuse you the gag because you're no longer an initiate, you've learnt control. You will contain your screams while I lash your thighs, your belly, your breasts. You will maintain the silence afterwards as I slide the handle into your soaking cunt. You will hold your breath until lightning forks the sky and a lilac blossom falls into the well of your navel. And only then, as your orgasm explodes, will you moan your release. Cradled in my arms again, you will weep your relief.

But you will cry again when you open your real present – which I will bring you on a tray with your morning coffee and croissant. I will throw open the shutters and the sun will stream in, shining on the gold wrapping paper you tear off the tiny box, glinting off the diamond you'll hold up in disbelief, sparkling a rainbow as I slide it onto your fourth finger.

Green Socks, White Lies

Just out of the shower on a Saturday morning, I rub lotion on my dry skin. Winter has arrived. "Pass me some socks, Leigh-Anne."

My daughter visits on weekends. At twelve, she studies my underwear drawer for clues on how to be a woman. She will get dull information from my bras and panties. "What colour?" she says.

"Any." There are no more Wonderbras, the garter belts are gone. The black lace-and-satin teddy I wore for her father was dumped in the garbage when I left him.

"What do you mean 'any'?" she asks, disbelieving. "Aren't you even going to try to match?"

All my undies want replacing. The bras have stretched, the socks have holes, and tiny filaments of elastic wave from the wrinkled edges of my knickers. Everything is grey from a thousand wash cycles. Without custody, there are no maintenance payments. My salary doesn't stretch to extras. Next birthday, my mother will send me a gift voucher for Woolies, but I will use it for groceries. "No matching; I'm wearing boots today."

She tosses me an apple-green sock ball, saying, "At least these will be out of sight then."

Like my underwear drawer, my make up tray is disappointing. She unscrews the stubs of lipstick smeared in cracked dispensers, and grimaces. The eye shadow from a long time ago lies cracked in dusty compacts. About twice a year I need mascara, and wave the sticky wand under warm water to loosen it. It suffices.

"Jayne wears pretty lacy G-strings," says Leigh-Anne. I wore them too when I was her father's plaything.

"Jayne is pretty," I say, trying to be generous to the woman who will offer my daughter a different role model.

"You really think so?" she asks, hopeful. I do not think so. Her cropped blonde hair and thick ankles are displeasing on the eye. Her power-dressing has an overbearing flavour of female chauvinism to

it. Her clear blue eyes and fresh complexion look like a mask
of vacuous sweetness to me. But now is not the time to be mean.
  "Sure!" Leigh-Anne's eyes light up. She hugs me tight.
The stepmother is good to her, packing her school lunch with love
letters attached to candy bars. I want to wish well this woman who
will finance my daughter's first leg wax, will teach her how to select
quality stretch-lace, and buy her first Clinique starter kit on her
thirteenth birthday. "Dad always liked pretty women."

Overture

Janina stood up in her front row seat at the end of the first act of *La Traviata*. She watched the musicians leaving the orchestra pit: the wind players were disassembled and dried their instruments; the trumpeters hung their horns from their music stands; the violinists loosened their bows.

A solid woman hooked her bow on the stand, lowered her double bass sideways and lifted long fingers to her head. She caught Janina's eye and winked as she released her wild blonde hair from a diamante clasp. It sprung in an unruly halo about her head for a moment before she twisted it back into the clasp. Janina stared at her cleavage and at the unlit cigarette fluttering between her lips. The bass player called loudly in Russian to someone waiting beyond the exit, took the cigarette between two slim fingers and blew Janina a kiss, before sauntering out.

Janina blushed in the dark, pulling away from the rail. After the blonde Russian had gone, she whisked out her camera phone, leaned down into the pit and took a photo of the double bass. She hurried to join Dave, her husband, who was exiting the auditorium. He hadn't noticed she wasn't following him.

"Let's head for the hills, babe," he said, when she touched his sleeve.

"Oh, please." Janina wanted to stay to the end, to watch Violetta dying in her beloved's arms. She wanted to see the blonde woman return, to watch her tune the bass and stroke her bow across the instrument, plucking the thick strings that reverberated deep and low.

"Aren't we even staying for drinks?" Perhaps the orchestra players would come out to order their drinks from the front of house.

"Nah! I'm beat. Tomorrow's a long day."

Janina fingered the staples binding the pages of the programme, feeling their sharpness cold against her fingers. She'd never seen a woman playing the double bass. Her husband tugged her sleeve, leading her towards the car park. She said, "You go, I'll get a taxi home later."

"No. Don't. Come home with me."

Dave sped home along De Waal Drive, tapping his fingers a-rhythmically on the steering wheel while Britney Spears simpered on the Audi's sound system. Janina felt an urge to grab the steering wheel, to force them to hit a tree. Instead she stuck her fingers in her ears. When Dave asked her what the matter was, she said she had a headache. "You seemed fine enough at the opera house," he said. She was trying not to cry.

Later in bed, Janina remembered Violetta's haunting aria, soaring over the bass's steady rhythm. She wondered if the bass player had really winked at her. The light hadn't been good. She might have imagined it. Same with the kiss she'd blown. Janina doubted and blushed again in the dark.

That night she dreamed she was stranded on a raft at sea, drifting out towards Robben Island. Sharks circled her and she felt light-headed. She was suffering from heatstroke. Instead of a water flask, she held a bottle of dishwashing liquid. Instead of an oar, she held a mop. Looking down at the raft, she realised she was adrift on a double bass, studded with diamonds.

The next morning after Dave left for work, she studied the programme, flipping to the back page, where the names of the orchestra players appeared by instrument. She dialled information. While waiting for the operator, she untwisted the staples and flicked them in the rubbish bin.

"Number for Goligorsky please," she said. Can't be many of them in Cape Town.

"Initial?"

"P, for Petrouchka."

Bionics

Sandwiches linger on a stainless steel platter in the recreation room of Harmony Home where my grandmother works. A net thrown over keeps flies off the food.

"Take one," says my grandmother, but the bread has splayed apart, revealing thick smears of institution margarine under dried out curls of ham.

I wave the flies away, saying, "No thank you, Gran," even though I am hungry and feeling faint.

A strong lemony antiseptic never quite covers the scent of piss, even in Gran's office where her cigarette smell is comforting. She is the matron. I need a quiet spot where I can study for my test tomorrow.

"What are you studying today?"

"*Love in the Time of Cholera.* It's our set work."

Gran shepherds me, like she does her patients, into the empty nurses' lounge where an abandoned cigarette balances on a silver ashtray.

"Sit here," she says, opening a window that lets in a fresh breeze. "Your mother will be here soon." I say, "Yes, Sister," as she leaves and then drag on the abandoned cigarette.

Some patients are visible in the next room. Most of them never wash their hands after they use the bathroom, even though my grandmother is always reminding them.

A woman with snapping dentures and lips the colour of beets hovers over the sandwiches. She scratches her head with fake nails, then fingers each one, peeking inside, looking for something she never finds. Around her wrist is a yellow armband that she plucks like a nervous tic.

A bearded guy with purple eyes says, "Help yourself and move along, Beryl."

She tells him she's researching the transfer of technology between life forms and synthetic constructs. He says, "Quit picking at the food, why don't you?"

She tells him that evolutionary pressure forces natural systems to become optimally efficient. A fly on the cast off netting rubs its legs together and I wonder how often the linen is laundered.

He says, "What would Jesus do?"

She looks at him as if to say, "Jesus would tell you to go fuck yourself," but murmurs instead, "I'm needed at the university."

He reaches for a wilted piece of parsley, holding it in one hand, offering it to her. With the other hand, he opens his trouser zipper, and touches himself.

Practise

I kiss my late mother-in-law's ring when I need help with her
difficult son – when he paces the house at night shouting at the rats
that aren't there, or panics, fearful that the floor is falling in, that the
roof is blowing off, that the neighbours are talking about him. I ask
her to send me an angel helper when I must calm him and put him
to bed.

I'm afraid that if I am in a car wreck, Merilyn's diamond will be
stolen from me while I lie unconscious; grave robbers before I'm
dead. I wonder if I should hide it in a safe. But when Linky's oupa
told the burglars that nobody had keys to the safe, that the house
had been bought ten years ago and the previous owners had lost the
key, and that there was nothing in the safe anyway, the guy with the
gold-capped tooth said, "We'll press you to talk, Oupa," and plugged
the iron in, good and hot.

After they seared his back and buttocks, Oupa shat himself and
his heart gave in. He died in his own excrement while they searched
his garage, fetched his wrench, his blowtorch. They ripped the safe
out the wall, bust it open, and found only dust and silence.

I love this ring too much not to wear it. I've told my family
to order an autopsy if I am murdered. Let a surgeon search my
stomach, because with my dying breath I will swallow this stone
whole. I practise slipping it off quickly – it's become a nervous tic.
My husband kisses my head when he sees me do that. "Don't drop
it down a grate," he says.

I remind him a thief will have to disembowel me for it.

Prognosis

Miss Dangerfield's legs dangled over the jetty at Lake Pleasant in the late afternoon sun. It was March and summer was dying. Her old feet looked like strange underwater flowers. She prodded the blue vein that coursed snake-like up her calf. She should talk about what the doctor had said, the medicine he'd prescribed, the prognosis. Over at the fire, Mrs Pinto slurped her whisky and soda. Sparks flew as she tossed on logs.

Mrs Pinto had wanted to stay at Pine Lake Marina, which offered a beauty spa and a tennis court, but Miss Dangerfield said the water-skiing was too noisy. Mrs Pinto grumbled that nothing exciting happened at Lake Pleasant, and the chalet was full of spiders, and the long grass full of ticks.

Just a Knysna Loerie's cry rang out. Lurid scarlet wings and a brilliant green body swooped over the water. The women sat together in silence for an hour.

After sunset, Mrs Pinto lifted the sosaties and boerewors onto the braai grid with knobbled hands. When a flame leapt up, Miss Dangerfield sprinkled it with beer. They debated whether to be adventurous and go to the Wild Coast. The potholes will wreck your tyres, said Miss Dangerfield, dabbing mosquito repellent onto her lover's forehead and ears. Let's stay here till Christmas, said Mrs Pinto, let's stay here forever.

New Word

Candice's father is a retired minister and my next-door neighbour. He sits with my baby girl on his lap, while I hand Candice the nappy bag containing Ally's bottles and disposables. She has just started to talk. She can say, 'Mama', 'juicy' and 'more'.

The old man interlaces his fingers in front of Ally and says, "Here is the church, here is the steeple . . ." Ally watches fascinated.

Candice was one of my first-year Education students last year. When I was 19, the age she is now, she played hopscotch on the pavement in front of my house. This year, she didn't return to campus. She stayed home to look after her father.

". . . open the doors and there are the people!" Ally laughs when the old man wiggles his fingers. He repeats the rhyme again and again.

Ally sticks her finger into the growth on Candice's father's head. He flinches, pulls away. It used to be a mole the size of a little pea. Then it became an acorn. Now it has a dimpled scab, like a chocolate golf ball. Every time it is cut away, it grows back bigger. Candice told me it's growing inwards now. He can't see properly anymore. His balance isn't good.

Ally reaches for the growth again. "Dirty," she says. It is a new word.

I blush. Candice looks away. The old man laughs, takes Ally's chubby hands in his and interlaces them. "Here is the church . . ."

I know he wants me to baptise her. Soon.

Goggles

Andrew persuaded Dad that the old geyser propped in the corner of the garage should be cut in half to make a first-rate braai grill. "Barbeque," said my mother, who refuses to use an Afrikaans word.

We drove over to Slang's place, Andrew, Dad and me, to borrow stuff for the project. Slang owns the Magalies Panel Beaters and his name suits him. Andrew needed an oxy-fuel cutter to get the pipes into equal lengths. He'd found them in the rubble behind the police station. The next stop was Oom Piet where they fetched a brazing torch to weld the pipe legs onto the casing. While we waited he popped pimples in the mirror on the back of the visor.

Back at home my brother said, "It will look good on the stoep."

"Veranda," said my mother. "It better not be ugly."

"We'll braai lamb chops and sosaties and wors," said my brother.

"We must buy charcoal," said Dad.

"You should invite Slang," said my mother, deliberately mispronouncing his name. She owes him because he fiddled her insurance last month when he fixed her car. We invited the neighbours whose African bluebells grow taller than ours. They're not bluebells, but my mother won't call them Agapanthus. I told her that that is the Latin name; it isn't Afrikaans, but it makes no difference.

The neighbours have two little kids, Mike and Ronnie, who are five and six and their noses always run.

"Something odd about them," says my mother. "Looks like they have foetal alcohol syndrome." Andrew reckons they were dropped on their heads.

I said, "They're sick again, they won't come."

"What ails them?" asked Dad.

"Cowpox," I said.

"Not possible," he said, backwashing into his fourth beer.
He leaned too close to the gas jet as they welded the legs onto the

braai. It singed his hair, making a vile smell that mixed with the gas from the brazing torch and the stink of molten metal. "Must be chicken pox," he said.

Andrew said, "They already had chicken pox. You can see the scars. You can't get it twice."

"Probably AIDS," said Dad. "They've got funny shaped heads."

The scars on Mike's arms and Ronnie's legs aren't from chicken pox. Their mother stubs out her cigarettes on them when they're naughty. I'm seven and smart and there's no point correcting my father wielding the blowtorch. If you knew their mother, you'd know it was cowpox.

Fan Mail

Dear Ms Sasha King,

My husband just presented me with a gift of your most recent CD for my birthday. I told him, "No chocolates this year, Buddy Brown. Chocolates are full of treacherous cholesterol. Do you want me to have a heart attack?"

Yesterday, I was 37, a conventional housewife, doing boring chores, used to sex in the missionary position – and, most significantly, I had never heard of Sasha King.

Today, at 38, I think I have been reborn. I have, and I hold, your newest album, 'The Boy Next Door'.

I took one look at the line-up of songs and I thought to myself, what class of chick sings guys' songs? I thought chocolate was hazardous. Hoo-whee! I didn't know there are significantly greater dangers under crêpe paper and satin ribbons than Côte d'Or could ever deliver.

It made no sense – the concept of a woman singing a man's song, that is. I didn't believe a gal could sing Frank Sinatra, Dave Brubeck, or Perry Como's love songs. It made no sense that the female voice would tackle lyrics made irresistible by the masculine aura of Sammy Davis Jr, Ray Charles and Louis Armstrong. Then I listened to your voice singing the words once sung by Dizzy Gillespie and Nat King Cole to the women they loved. I suddenly realised. You are no ordinary kind of woman.

I'm listening to you sing 'Too Darn Hot', and I feel my nipples tingling. 'Makin' Whoopee' makes my clit start to throb. I'm enchanted. Captivated. Enthralled. I Got It Bad too, Ms King. This music should come with a warning label.

Today I am looking at your picture on the case and inside the booklet. I can't get you out of my mind. I am a changed woman, and I am holding you responsible. Today, I realise that The Boy Next Door just doesn't do it for me any more. It isn't a boy I want any longer – not that I particularly wanted one before –and looking at your elfin features, your laughing face, your long thin arms, your edible toes, I realise it is a girl I now desire. Never before did I even look at girls, but I'm looking at what there is to see now. Right now.

It's you I desire. Ooh-Shoo-Be-Doo-Bee – I do, I do!

Now, please understand, I'm not one to write fan letters to anybody. But then again, you are not anybody. No, I'm sure you are an incarnation of Freya. I've been reading a book on the goddesses, and you'll be interested to hear that Freya didn't discriminate in her choice of lovers. That's a right, gods and goddesses alike were fair game. How about that? Freya and Frigga are the two aspects of the great goddess. Freya was the maiden, Frigga, the mother.

Do you realise that in all four pictures printed, you don't look once at the camera? Why would that be, Ms King? Are you truly demure?

Do you hide your eyes because you realise the effect you have on people? I can tell that my husband would like to ball you. He looks lecherously at your chiffon skirt that reveals so much fine thigh. He figures you are a lesbian dyke who just needs a good schlong where a schlong fits best. He would like to rip those feathery garments off you and give it to you good. Maybe he bought the CD so that he might perve over you too. I didn't ask. Until yesterday I was a boring housewife stuck in the missionary position. Maybe I will ask, though.

But wait – another question before you quit. Did you anticipate the response you would evoke in women? Did you know what you would do to me? Is that why you avert your gaze?

Can I tell you that I would like to look into your eyes? Not just at a photo, but right into your eyes, as I unstrap those simple, elegant sandals of yours. I want to watch your expression change as I massage your instep, as I rub the ball of your foot with a deep, steady pressure. I want to see your mouth open as I trail my fingers through your short, cropped hair, trailing my little finger along the curves of your ear. I want to see if you smile as I remove the voile blouse you wear, and untie your beaded corset. I want to see you blush, perhaps stare away, as I hold your breasts in my hands, sucking your nipples.

Don't be afraid. This is where it begins and ends, Ma'am. I Got It Bad, but I'll recover. Of course I will. I'm not ready to throw out the husband on account of your pretty hands, your demure little breasts. Don't be afraid. I'm no stalker. The truth is, I don't even know which capital of the world you inhabit. I'm guessing you're a Brit, because you are so classy. And because the album was recorded in London. But singing American music, you would do it with the right accent. You're The Top, after all.

Don't worry, I'm not going to follow you, or even send you pesky emails. I'm not going to make a complete ass of myself, behaving like a teenage dolt swooning over a pop star. Would you believe that I don't even know how to surf the Internet? My kids help me if I need to know something – like a recipe or a guide for planting by the moon. I understand that, in theory, I could get a picture of you from the World Wide Web; I could get an email back from your fan club.

Oh no, Sasha King, I won't though. That's not nearly good enough for you – or me. This fan mail is confidential correspondence. It serves my housewifely need to put pen to paper, to keep private my unexpected yearning, to offer me maximum pleasure with minimum fuss. Besides, I have always managed without you. The proposal is that I Get Along Without You Very Well from now on too.

You see, pretty lady, you gave me so much more than music. You gave me a whole new world, a world where a girl can make love to a smoky-voiced girl. I knew it was possible, but I never gave it very much thought. But you've given me an idea of how it might be, and so, here, in my private diary, I can write my beautiful fantasy.

Say It Isn't So!

I shall buy myself roses, light candles, run a deep, scented bath. Alone, I shall open a chilled bottle of wine. I shall turn on your voice and soap my breasts. I shall tease my nipples, thrust my fingers between my legs. Sasha King, don't worry about me.

All I Do Is Dream Of You.
Once I have climaxed, and rested, I shall start again.
The Best Is Yet To Come.

Lollipop

Mr Wall stood under the tree at Mostert's Mill with his back to us so we wouldn't see him sneaking a smoke. What we did see, with his foot resting on a low knoll in the trunk, was the outline of his briefs pulled taut across his perfect buttocks under khaki chinos.

Susannah told us he'd switched his brand of cigarettes. I said Camels gave him donkey breath. Ankara giggled. Susannah said it didn't, but that's because she wants to shag him. I know because she wrote a graffiti heart with his and her names on the toilet door.

The fat lady tour guide, who was explaining how they climb the ladder to put up the windmill sails, stopped her talk and scowled at us. Mr Wall ground out his cigarette and wandered back, standing right behind us for the rest of the talk.

Before we got on the bus we bought strawberry lollipops. I made slurping sounds all over mine and whispered to Ankara, "What am I sucking now?" Ankara giggled because she knew exactly what I meant, and she said I'd better not because Mr Wall has AIDS.

"How'd you know?" I asked.

"He wears a red ribbon on his jacket. All people with AIDS have to wear that ribbon."

I said that was crap. All the teachers wear it and they're not sick. Susannah started to cry and I felt kak because I'd forgotten her father died last year from cancer, but everyone knows the real reason why.

Sun-Dried Tomatoes

My mother hangs droopy carrots on the clothesline with snapping pegs. If I challenge her she says they are orange socks. But it is clear to our neighbours passing by: nothing is normal in our house any more. Most people no longer stare over our wall at the old motor car abandoned on bricks. Weeds have climbed through the chassis out of the windows since my father went away. Passers-by cross to the other side at the top of the road and back again at the bottom to avoid witnessing my mother as she plants father's socks and shirts in the vegetable patch. Mother says they cross the street because the drains leak outside our gate, but nobody in this neighbourhood likes to see tomatoes and peppers flapping in the breeze.

Under my SAPS Star

At Diepkloof's Aliens Investigation Unit a kindly captain
recovered my heart from the defunct fountain. Alerted by an
uncommon rustling while she filed a repatriation report she knew
immediately whose heart it was. So pale, so under-developed it could
only be a white girl's heart. And she knows hearts, that full-breasted
captain.

She told me she often finds lost ones on the train to Mozambique.
Illegal aliens lose them all the time at Johannesburg station. But
black folks' hearts are big, she said holding her hands apart, the size
of a dinner plate.

And so I love that captain who held my heart under warm water,
washing away the cigarette butts, the lizard shit and fallen leaves.
With gentle fingers she unbuttoned my blue blouse. You must be
more careful, Constable. She lifted my left breast, pale as pap.
The State will not be held responsible for such silliness in future.

She slotted my loss back into the tiny hole where it beats now
under tender black fingerprints. Where she patted my SAPS star
back in place my misshapen ventricles pump, yearning for her touch.
My buttons quiver, my nameplate shakes.

I salute her on parade with a restless longing. Like a deportee
planning an illicit return, my little heart holds a sliver of hope.

Beached

After a southern right whale washes up on Mnandi Beach the fat
boy can no longer sketch the chocolate girl who always sits facing
him at the Ocean of Paradise Café. He's watched her for
a month now, with a soft pencil in his hand, observing how she bows
her head after the waitress places her food on the table. She'll stop
talking to the umbrella woman for the subtlest pause, placing her
hands in her lap and closing her eyes. Then she takes up her knife
and fork, organising her plate.

He's watched how she chews with quick, precise movements of
her full lips, and how she uses both hands to wipe her mouth with
a paper serviette. Once she sent her plate back, sniffing and gesturing
at the peas. The manager offered a refund. She smiled and nodded.
It's been easy to watch her because she stares only at the umbrella
woman sitting across the table. When he's tried to draw other
people, they notice him and get cross. They move away. But the
chocolate girl hasn't seen him. She makes him feel as small as a shell.

If the fat boy could finish just one painting of her, he'd give it to
her. Just give it. He wouldn't ask a bean.

He thinks about taking her photograph so that he could complete
the sketches at home but she eats so fast, he never finishes drawing
before she's gone. Every day she returns to the coffee shop and he
starts a new one. If he could take photographs of her, he'd focus on
the great buckle on her handbag that she swings over the back of her
chair. Or he'd study the coffee-gold weave of the wrap draped over
her shoulders, the delicate straps around her crossed ankles below her
chair. But it would scare her, to have him lying on the floor beside
her chair with a camera, heaving and sighing at her sandals.

The fat boy watches her down at the visitor's centre, where she
hands out pamphlets and gives directions on the phone. At closing
time she locks the doors and he follows her down to the beach,
watches her slip off her heels, tracing her footprints, wondering how

to draw them.

He stands behind her in the crowd that has gathered around the whale to help the Police and Navy divers trying to refloat it. He is close enough to touch her when she screams at a child that has begun to kick the creature. He only looks when the umbrella woman leads her away, crying, because a policeman is weighing down the explosive device upon the whale's blowhole with a sandbag.

That's not how he wants to paint her. He wants to catch her at the restaurant table, with her eyes closed and her head turned upward, as the umbrella woman brushes a strand of damp hair sticking to her dark brown cheek. He wants to capture that moment like a prayer in oils on canvas so that he becomes like her. But now when he lifts his pencil, he sees only blubber and blood.

Deities

Josie's screen saver is the plum-brown cottage on the edge of an inlet, somewhere in British Columbia. The first plume of fall is reflected in the surface of the water, orange leaves on a single tree. The other trees in the image are still a sober, dark green. She remembers the stillness, autumn scents of cinnamon and apple, cider she'd tasted for the first time.

If she taps her keyboard, the headlines will intrude. Grim news: Another family attacked by thieves who raped the woman in front of her husband and son, torturing the father with a hot iron, demanding his bank card code. In another part of town, a pensioner walking his dog was shot for his mobile.

Her visualisation is part of her plan to manifest an escape, but now she can't remember exactly where she took the photo. She hopes the deities won't mind, but forgetting feels somehow irresponsible. Intentions should be specific. Ask for what you want.

The day she'd visited that cottage on the inlet, she'd held a smooth pale stone from the water's edge, so unlike the gold silk sand of the beaches she knows. She threw the stone into the slate grey depths and it fell with a plop, its ripples spreading further and further. She imagined them travelling across the oceans, into the southern hemisphere, merging with the waves that crashed onto the beach at Mtunzini, where sand crunches underfoot in the humidity, and only flowers are orange, never leaves. Leaves are only ever brilliant green, emerald, jade and lime.

The clapboard cottage was in a calm cold place. She whispers to the image: "Take me there. I'll learn to walk in snow; I'll even love the ice."

She read that if you put enough energy into your intentions, they continue working behind the scenes even if you forget about them; like residual rehearsals for a night crossing.

On a turquoise sky day when the waves thrash silver against the beach, Josie throws a dozen red roses into the surf, calling on her ancestors: *Oupa Keith, guide us; Ouma Millie, guard our money; Grandpa Reggie, help our visas; Granny Pat, watch the girl-child; Ma Merilyn, mind the boys . . .*

The rising tide and onshore wind dump the roses back on the beach, rejecting her prayers. Josie gathers them up, wading again into the warm pounding water, and flings them back, shouting into the wind, "We can't stay here any more. Please don't make us stay." The cross-tide sends the blooms, battered and bruised, further down the beach where a girl gathers them in a dripping bunch.

Josie strides down the beach, intending to say, Hey, you can't take those. They're sacred offerings. Throw them back. She imagines the mother seeing her wild-haired and wide-eyed, crazy. She anticipates her pulling her daughter toward her protectively. She stops when she notices just one lonesome bloom bobbing beyond the breakers.

She sits in the soft sand, her heart hammering, her breath ragged. Maybe it's enough.

Saviour

The tramp who sleeps in the church garden trudges past our house at 5.42 a.m. each day. His dragging limp and the bang of his walking stick are my alarm clock. Sometimes he wakes me with his sorrowful tune: 'On Jordan's Stormy Banks I Stand'. Other times I'm already waiting for him, my own wailing hymn bouncing off the half-finished mural in the baby's room.

At night I fall asleep quickly after the supper I cook but can't eat, but I wake frequently from nightmares of drowning. I slide out of bed, and wait for morning beside the cot, lit by the greenish light from the street.

Joe began painting the mural last summer after he'd felt the first kicks. He started with a cluster of stylised stars hovering over a windmill in a field, with mealies and mice and sunflowers. He said his inspiration was the scenic route to Vereeniging.

"There is no scenic route to Vereeniging," I said.

"Don't be argumentative," he said. "It's a metaphor. Vereeniging means Unity. We're going to be a family at last."

A week later the kicking stopped. "No heartbeat," said the intern on duty at the emergency room that smelled like fear and cleaning fluid.

Joe never completed the happy scarecrow he'd practised in his sketchbook in pencil crayon. I trace its outlines with my finger till I'm cold and stiff. One night while I sleep Joe paints over the stars and scarecrow. When I awake, I grope along the wall, trying to remember where the scarecrow's unfinished heart was, where his floppy hat should be. The mealie fields are gone. The stars have been put out. The blank wall is an icy sea and my lungs are filled with salt.

When the tramp limps past our window at 5.42 a.m. singing, 'Wade in the Water' I walk out and follow him.

One Hundred Babies

Madiba invites me to enter the well at dusk. He gives me a lily, a cross and a drum; and his good wishes. He takes my hands in his and says, "Be strong. Our country needs your work." If I complete one hundred quilts before dawn, all the orphans with AIDS will be well.

The well is an ammonite, curling into the dark; a tunnelling of fabrics, and I am eager to serve. But a single quilt can take a year, can take twenty-seven.

In the first chamber, bales of solid cotton heaped in organised stacks are in colours of peanut and clay brick, soil and sunset. The scents of calico and chintz are crushed wheat; the rich soft corduroy, sweet chocolate sods. The babies will be warm under my quilts: Sunshine and Shadows, and Building Blocks. But I need pastels and primary colours for Baby Bow-Tie, rainbow shades for Little Buddy, not earth tones, not winter.

In the next chamber the prints flow crazily off their rolls: floral and check, paisley and polka dots; a shambles of mauve and fire, bruises and orange. Some quilts have been started and others are almost done. No time to order or sort. I pick up the incomplete sewing of other seamstresses. Sloppy seams tell of hurried work. Corners don't intersect. Colours don't match. Fingers racing, I might be able to complete just one before the night is done, but other needlewomen failed here too. They did not begin at the centre.

In the next room, the fabrics have been disturbed. Taffetas in sorry shades are overturned; velvets in despair are strewn about. The room is a swirl of bleak sheens and blistering light: stressed concrete and winter haze, mining disasters and quarry glare. These will not do for Pink Lemonade and Bright Garden.

Down a level, quickening my step, past tools and materials; set squares and rotary blades, templates cut from x-rays, patterns designed on old report cards, sewing machines and quilting looms.

Pre-cut shapes tower in wobbling piles of spun sugar squares, triangles of fruit and hexagons of petals. But I must sort out the unfamiliar shapes: hexagons and dodecahedrons, unsuitable for Little Buddy and Wiggle Flowers.

When the clock strikes midnight, I rush through a room where beads and buttons and sequins become freckles and eyes and tears. I hurry, grabbing needles and thimbles, more than I can carry, planning patterns in my head: Play Mates for the girls, Sunny Sailors for the boys.

Chamber after chamber, and still I carry the lily, cross and drum. The stairs are stitches going down, down, down. Basting and slip stitch, blanket stitch for appliqué. If I go far enough I'll find the centre, the place from where I must begin. But the hours accelerate, the babies' breaths are shallow, their whimpers echo down the well.

One hundred quilts or they will all die. The sky, a long way up is turning orange. The ibis shrieks to greet the sun. No good fairies appear, nor wizened crones. The quilts don't piece themselves together and I can't silence that first bird.

The lily, the cross and the drum were never meant for the quilts. In the middle of the ammonite is the old man's pick and shovel. Earth and lime, waiting for one hundred tiny caskets.

Vessel

Make a pinch pot every day. It's the simplest thing, the hardest.
Don't wait for passion or vision. Or bouquets of inspiration. Expect
monotony. You will be bored, like you were as a kid, when you
practised limping scales on that reluctant piano. You always curled
your thumbs too late, displacing the rhythm.

You are a beginner again, learning the limits. Motivation won't
appear until you do. It might not appear anyway, but start with the
clay – one glob fitting well in your hand. Roll it in a ball. Dip your
thumb in the middle to form the centre. You might want to put it
on your nose, like a clown, hoping for a diversion to alleviate the
nothingness you feel. But don't. It will spoil the shape.

Rotate the ball, pinching as you go, to even out the emptiness.
Keep an even thickness in the walls. Do it daily because your life
depends on it. It's not a hollow gesture. Reach for that perfect form
in this simple task. Do not curl your thumb too soon. Take time.
Gently pat the bottom on a flat surface. For stability.

Once your daily pot is done, then be ambitious. Mould a stallion
rearing from a pedestal. Or coil a giant urn for a corporate client,
rolling long cool snakes, scratching each surface with a red plastic
fork. Moisten the cross hatches, blend and stroke.

Or try a nude: form a short thick snake for a flaccid penis;
devoting your good eye to the glans. Laugh when you realise how
your tongue hangs out as you fondle his balls, cupping them like
a lover.

Next day roll another lump, make another pinch pot. Don't skip
this step. How else will you press your emptiness into substance?
Do it every day, this pulling of something from nothing. Don't rush.
Keep each pot on your windowsill. At month end select the most
nearly perfect one for the kiln. Return the imperfections
to the sludge where you will wedge them another day. At the end
of the year, glaze the only one that did not keen or wilt or slope

in the firing.

Every ten years, select the most nearly round pot, throwing the rest away lest they become holders of stale garlic, paper clips, old mints. When your days are almost done, lodge the best pot at the crematorium. You will be familiar with the inside of the furnace.

You will not be afraid. And when you've been fired, your gritty remains of bone and ash will fill that hollow you perfected once with your thumbs.

Catch the Bouquet

The hydrangea blooms on the west side of the bushes are every lush shade from purple to blue. Protected by the afternoon shadow of the house, they retain their colour like reticent bridesmaids, away from the glare of speculation and gossip. On the east side of the bushes, the morning light has burned the blossoms, leaving them pale as work shirts in the laundry basket, their tips covered in brown blisters like rust spots hissing from a steam iron the new bride forgot to empty. The leaves below are cool and thick, their veins protected. The new bride hides in the shadow of the house. With her bum on the grass and her back to the wall she is invisible from inside. She strokes the wooded stalks, the unspoiled blooms temporary between her fingers as the lilac-ribboned favours at the reception, wishing now she'd worn the bridesmaid's dress instead.

Aromas

The tables at Aromas are cleanish and don't rock and you can see a sliver of sky between the tatty awnings if you work for it. A flat screen TV the size of a swimming pool shows fashion models in bathing costumes. How can I eat watching hungry girls? Even with the sound way down their stomachs rumble. The manager is clueless.

With my back to the TV, I watch a man in baggy sweatpants and stained t-shirt chew with his mouth open. He can never be satiated because those feline creatures poised to leap from the screen stalk his dreams instead of waiting at his door, ready to rip off his yarmulke and sink their claws into his beard, scratching and hissing as they devour him.

I eavesdrop on the next table, hearing one-sided fragments between two mismatched women.

What it was, the divorce . . . cheated the money . . . because Mamzo is so lovely . . . she does favours . . . sure, a challenge . . . the way is open . . .

The loud-voiced one faces away, wearing a leopard print blouse and wide afro. She never finishes a sentence. I jot down the fragments on a napkin, wondering at the blanks.

The waitress brings chicken schnitzel, coleslaw with wodges of mayonnaise and cherry tomatoes, not quite red. I eat without relish. A tomato skids off my plate, landing beneath Mr Yarmulke's chair. I spike the next tomato with more precision. It squirts seeds over the back of my hand, which I suck off, wishing Mr Yarmulke were watching me instead.

The chicken is fatty. Once it's too late, I realise this bird will cluck a tart refrain along my oesophagus during my meeting, startling away my clever questions, leaving me off-centred and unhinged. I will wish I were hungry instead of bloated. I will suck an antacid and burp discreetly.

Mamzo will explain the . . . Doreen is jealous of . . . The day that choir . . . Salt for the wounds . . .

The older woman looks like a nun with a heavy silver cross and rough haircut. She nods and chews while her companion talks, but her eyes stray to the bikini girl on the catwalk. She responds to her companion in monosyllables, her jaw barely moving when, but when she looks at the TV, she licks her lips.

I try to catch the waitress's eye, but she's focused on the back of her arm, squeezing blackheads single-handed. The mismatched women rise and pass. I scrunch up the napkin and toss it in my empty coffee mug. The woman in the alligator shoes puts her hand on the nun's shoulder.

Mamzo has experience as . . .Doreen won't . . . come to mishap . . .

I twist open my blood red lipstick and apply it behind my hand, then slip the pepper grinder into my handbag. I undo my top buttons to reveal my teal bra strap and walk slowly to Mr Yarmulke's table, telling him in a husky voice that I've mislaid my pepper grinder, ask to borrow his. When he says, Yes, I say, My tomato has rolled under your seat . . .

Petting

Dizzy, the bird of my heart, a honey-breathed Pionus flew away last Christmas when the rain was boiling and the lightning kicked. She left me just one feather at the bottom of her cage: salmon coloured, with shimmery petrol-green tints. I tuck it in my bra on days when I feel low and my husband's parrot is nibbling his earlobe. I visit Dobbin's Dogs and Birds. The saleslady tries to sell me the snake that's woven through her coiffure. "Does it hiss?" I ask. "Only when I eat apples," she says. She promises there are four Pionus chicks in the nest; she will call me in a few days to fetch my baby bird. I phone when she doesn't call. She tells me the mother killed the babies; she didn't have the heart to call with bad news. My husband's parrot thinks she is his wife and I am mistress scum. When I bend to kiss him, she pecks open my cheek.

Button

We called her Miss Fabulous, although her real name was Miss Fabaldon, because when she checked your writing or listened to your reading, she would touch you on the shoulder and say, "Those are fabulous kicking kings you've written today, Nzuzo." Or she'd take your hand and look you in the eye saying, "You read like a superstar, Moses." Her eyes were the colour of melted chocolate, her arms the colour of milk. She would share the pickle from her sandwich with me. It made my heart flutter.

The choir sang at her wedding, so some of us got to see her new husband, Mr Rumboll. He was short, much shorter than she, but when he took her hands in his, she seemed to become tiny and disappear. At the organ, the music teacher rendered 'Love Divine, All Loves Excelling', and we remembered to breathe deeply, to support with our diaphragms, to drop our jaws, to enunciate each word clearly. We sang our hearts out for Miss Fabulous.

By the end of the year her eyes were more the colour of discarded coffee grounds, and she would forget to eat her sandwich, even when I asked her about the pickle. She started wearing scarves around her neck, and long sleeves. Once I peeked through her blouse where a button had popped open. I saw her breast under her lacy bra. Her skin wasn't like milk anymore, more like yellow green stains. When we read to her she would say, "Good," in a flat voice. When she marked our writing, she'd write, Nice. When Moses called her Mrs Grumble behind her back, I started to cry. She never touched us on our shoulders anymore. Once, I hugged her, but she pushed me away saying, "Ow, kiddo, be careful!"

Infectious

A woman waited in doorways, stood under arches, listened
at windows for the magical abracadabra – a combination she knew
would arrive.

The doctor said it could come at any given time, so she listened
to the September wind, waited for Jacaranda blossoms to fall
and pop underfoot in November. Hadedas shrieked at dawn in
December, but by February there was still no sign, only sighs and
post gathering unopened on the mantel, her nails chewed till they
bled and throbbed.

The taxi driver with flared nostrils said it would come soon.

It would be a cryptic code; the right words whispered by
a stranger wearing lilac eyeshadow perhaps: light of lime, purge
of pipe. Or a message flashing on an electronic hording over the
highway: inner circle infant, don't drop the dog.

How will I know if I've been called, she asked at confession?
The priest said to open last year's umbrella. She consulted a palm
reader, a gambler, a hungry vagrant to whom she'd given a tin
of beans. She offered up her questions to those who would take
them, gave them away for free.

The radio bumped onto the indigenous language station by
accident. In that moment of wondering what language she was
hearing: Tsonga or Venda? The DJ spoke the answer in a leeched
voice: answer your phone, please and dammit, or at least open
your post.

Cooking

Knock, knock, are you hot?
Reply or die, what's the cry?
Ooh! Ah! Ja, o ja!
If you do, don't tell your ma."

The junior girls are French-skipping next to the netball court,
elastic firm around their skinny knees, gymslips flying with each
hop and twist. On the court, the seniors practise for today's netball
quarter-final. They jostle for the ball. Catch. Two steps. Throw.
Pleated skirts swing revealing firm thighs, taut buttocks, little breasts
jiggle with each pitch and shoot. Catch. Two steps. Throw. This
afternoon the boys will come to the match, honking vuvuzelas,
whistling and waiting. Hungry plucky boys. When I was ten
we sang:

Chocolate cake when you bake,
how many minutes do you take?

Smarts

Our picture appears on the school magazine's winners' page:
Top Three Excel in Thailand. And in the *Greenside Gazette*:
Whiz Kids Do It Again. Pa nods and nods. Ma, glowing, says,
"Shenaaz Cachalia, you and your friendlies, you all is right beauts."
But with her dentures are floating in a tub on the sink it sounds like
we are 'light beets'.

The Jada girl has high teeth. Her braces should pull them down
in time, but the tracks bulge beneath her lips which form a perpetual
wince. It's a toss-up where to look when she talks. Do I avoid
following her lazy eye? Or do I try not to stare at her big mouth?

The Tokolia boy is a dwarf with a protruding forehead like
a pumpkin and flappy arms that don't keep still. Nothing can fix that
barrel of afflictions.

And me with my African bum – vast haunches you can settle a tea
pot on, my breasts, a shelf for the milk jug and sugar bowl – I diet
and diet, but my flesh stays put.

At the prize giving in Jakarta, the Tokolia boy wore a mustard suit
made especially by his dressmaker aunt. The Jada girl was in a carrot-
coloured dress with white spots like fraying aspirins. Her one eye is
on the camera, the other on my aubergine two-piece with diagonal
stripes that were supposed to draw the eye away from my fuller
figure. I'm holding the trophy we won at the International Maths
Symposium.

Oprah says in her magazine, "Learn to Love your Perfect Flaws".
But she doesn't say what you should do when graffiti reappears on
the toilet walls: Top Three Still Ugly Muslim Devils.

The Corner of My Eye . . .

. . . is an unreliable square, a questionable source of information,
where leaves turn to scorpions, sticks to skeletons and blossoms
to flames. When I turn to stare full on, there is no ostrich,
but a black bag, persecuted and stuffed with rubbish, no neck,
but a mop mocking my insecurity. Beneath my feet are stones
not bread. How could I be confused when only pebbles rattle this
underfoot rhythm? Yet glass eyeballs do so too. I should like to pass
a boulder in this wasteland and be sure it is not a backpack, because
no fisherman casts a line in this desert, no farmer ploughs this field.
Only an owl alights on a rock to hoot derision at my need for fresh
water, not waves. I wish the corner of my eye was round, like my
longing for the moon.

Mr Fixit's Lament

My father, recently retired, flies into Johannesburg Airport on free Voyager Miles, with spanners in his suitcase, a voltmeter in his hand luggage and tap washers in his top pocket. I have forestalled the plumber with a bucket under the cistern to catch the slow leak that started right after Dad's last visit. And I have staved off the electrician by not running the oven and the bedroom heaters at the same time.

Like I did when I was a girl, I pass him tools, hold one end of the measuring tape and stabilise the ladder. I learn the respective purposes of gland screws and grub nuts, rediscover mole grips and shifting spanners, and ask about drill bits and plug cutters. Dad's purple-tinted veins protrude from the back of his hands where liver spots have appeared that didn't exist before. I look at my own hands, fingers splaying just like his. My thumbs are also solid, unyielding and my knuckles bear his genetic imprint.

When my father flies home, the toilet behaves again, and the taps, not the electrics, will sparkle. We've saved a grand, but our retired playmate grumbles into his G&T at the airport bar. He says we kept him from wild women and the casino. I say, Pop, your wild woman is waiting for you in Cape Town.

On the M2 homeward bound, my husband looks hangdog. I stare at his hands gripping the steering wheel – hands that know the landscape of the piano like a mystic weatherman, finding chords and keys by feel. His thumbs rain the repetitive rhythm of shaded accompaniments; pass over the notes, pick scales, pluck melodies from the keyboard like a conjurer. He rests one hand on his leg. Freckles and fine ginger hairs catch the sunlight coming through the windscreen. I reach over to stroke it. It is the hand that rests on my belly at night, that ruffles my hair, scratches my back, stirs my coffee and makes the sandwiches I take to work.

My husband sighs, wishing he could replace gutters and remedy

138

sagging shelves or coax an ornery kettle into submission. But pianists understand the mechanics of uneven rhythm, unstable harmony. They know about texture and balancing dynamics, suspending a cadence, accelerating a climax.

I remind my musician how he found the slivers of my betrayed heart, picked them up, held them tenderly while I buried old roles: scapegoat, scarlet woman, parish pariah.

Custody-cheated I mourned my children, while, with meticulous care, my best boy pieced the fragments of my heart back together. I tell him again how he seamed them, sang them – slowly, beautifully back in place.

Idioms

One snowy December we move from Connecticut to Gaborone. Mom's stomach is round as a pumpkin. She puts my hands on her belly, letting me feel the baby kick. Botswana is the hottest sandiest dump you ever saw. We rent a house in Broadhurst while our new place is being built in Phakalane, the golf estate. Dad says we've found paradise. Property here is dirt cheap. But Mom starts talking to strangers, lingering in the street without a hat. She tells an old woman passing by, "You're voting with fire."

In the hardware shop she fills her basket with nails and pliers and says to the cashier, "It's a baptism by forklift." Dad reckons the dust is addling her brain. She needs help. He hires Regomoditswe to clean the house, but nobody can pronounce her name so we call her Reggie. She teaches me the Tswana greetings: 'Dumela, Ma' when she arrives and 'Tsamaya sintle' when she leaves. She makes chotlo, chopping the meat fine, removing the bones. She says, "In our culture, this dish is a treat for the toothless."

Mom lies on the cool kitchen floor stroking the concrete. She says over and over, "Redemption comes in small packages." Dad finds her there when he returns from work. He helps her up, brushing the dust from her cheek. She tells him, "A birth in the hand is worth two in the bush."

Unpronounceable

Sherezade's mouth knew words I couldn't pronounce, let alone spell. While our aunts folded samoosas, fried chilli bites, and chopped the sambals for the biryani simmering in heavy pots, my cousin and I explored the big house. Our fathers and uncles had all gone to watch our brothers play cricket, so we had plenty of time on our hands.

"Do you know where your humerus is?" she asked.

"Of course," I lied. "It's your funny bone."

"I'm going to show you," she said.

Uncle Mohammed, Sherezade's father, had a skeleton in his surgery with a screw that attached the skull to a stand on wheels. Sherezade showed me the funny bone, pulling the arm up by the fingers.

"See here, how the capitulum unites with the radius at the elbow and the trochlea is a notch, joining the ligament to the head of the ulna."

I listened to the strange words which sounded like poems. Her hand rested lightly on my upper arm, stroking the fabric of my sleeve. She leaned in close and said, "Here is your humerus."

Sherezade's older sister, Fatima, was away at university, so we sneaked her portable record player into her father's study and put the Beatles on. We sang along, at the top of our voices, wiggling the stand until the bones jived and clattered rudely:

'Oh please, say to me, you'll let me be your man,

And please, say to me you'll let me hold your hand . . .'

"I'm going to show you something else," said Sherezade, unpacking a plastic model of the human heart. She taught me about valves and ventricles and explained the difference between veins and arteries. Then she snapped the box shut, and returned it to her father's drawer, taking his cigarettes and minty chewing gum from under a stack of papers.

"What happens when Uncle-ji discovers them gone?" I asked, giggling into my palm.

"Papa will think Mama found his latest hiding place and then he'll find another."

We slipped into the tin shed beyond the blue gum trees to smoke. Inside were the old horse blankets from before the equine flu. The State Veterinarian had instructed Uncle Mohammed to shoot all his horses. We lay on the blankets watching sunbeams in the dappled light that smelled of leather and eucalyptus. I couldn't tell if it was the memory of my uncle weeping over the horses or if Sherezade unplaiting my braid made the sky seem bluer and the air hotter.

We stubbed out our cigarettes and opened our gum. Sherezade rested her hand on my calf, caressing my knee then inching up my thigh.

"Do you know where your areola is?" asked my cousin in a voice as smooth as newly opened poppy petals.

I nodded even though I didn't. I held my breath as her hand searched the embroidered folds of my tunic, finding an opening. She stroked my belly, then reached for my nipple. I jumped as she pinched it, but not from pain.

"Is . . ." I hesitated. "Is this . . . not wrong?"

"No. You are perfect," she said, spitting out her gum. "This skin around your nipple, *that* is your areola, and it is very good."

I thought to ask her about the will of Allah, but as she was already licking that puckering skin, it seemed like interrupting a conversation. I wanted to know so many things: could one tell whether Uncle Mohammed's skeleton had been a man or a woman? Did the State Veterinarian have a horse skeleton in his consulting room? What would it take for my breasts to smell like mint forever?

Tune Song

As soon as her mother puts in her teeth, the whistling starts, and Karien can tell how the day will be. The breathy chirruping is an aural weather vane, predicting an outcome. Whatever the tune, if it swoops like a swallow on a curved flight path and lands precisely at the anticipated point, then the day is sparkly and light.

More and more, since her mother moved a year ago into the granny suite attached to their house, the whistling flounders: the melody goes off key, or her mother can't reach the high notes. The rhythm stalls and the day veers off course. Her mother forgets the endings of songs, then loops round to the beginning, trying over and over to arrive at the final cadence. When that happens, Karien braces herself for a day of lost keys, fingers slammed in doors and sandwiches half made and not eaten.

Because her mother can't stand to not finish a tune, she improvises an ending even as she tries to remember it.

"Let it go, Ma," says Karien when her mother stops at the eggs in the supermarket, eyebrows furrowed. But the old woman's claw-like fingers are in her ears, not so much to shut out the muzak but to call up the notes that have fluttered out of range. Karien taps her mother's shoulder, startling her.

"Sh! I'm trying to get the whole tune in my head again," she says, stepping backwards and bumping into a woman with a loaded basket. "I need to get to the end; I must have closure."

The melody is gone. For the rest of the day little else will be right either. The heels of the old lady's socks will slide down, forming lumps in her shoes, her laundry will fold skew and topple over as she puts it in her drawer. Even her towel will hang off kilter and fall to the floor.

Karien takes her mother along to fetch the children from school, hoping the distraction will relieve the tension. She plays *La Rondine* on the car radio. Maybe Puccini will chase the tune away for good.

Karien's children slope out the gate and fling their rucksacks into the boot, then slump on to the back seat, landing so hard that the car rocks.

"We can axe that, can't we?" says her daughter, leaning between the front seats to switch off the opera, not waiting for her mother's permission. She kisses her grandmother's cheek. As soon as the speakers emit the small hiss of the sound shutting off, Kariena's mother starts whistling. The other occupants of the car sigh collectively.

"Should I switch it back on?" says the girl.

"Leave it," says Karien.

"You like that tune, don't you, Gran?" says her daughter with the triple ear piercing that defies school rules. There is the slightest edge of facetiousness to the girl's tone. Karien wants to believe that her daughter is asking questions because if the old lady is talking she can't whistle.

"What are you whistling, Gran?" says her son.

"Just a tune song."

He laughs, saying, "Not a *choon*, Gran. You're whistling a *tune*."

"Oh ho?" says the old lady, "That's what I just said, a choon song."

"Say tune, Grandma, say tuna, say t-t-t. Your tongue must touch the tip of your teeth."

Her daughter says, "A tune song is a tautology. It's either a tune, or it's a song. Both is redundant."

"Both *are* redundant," says her son.

Karien's own tongue slouches at the back of her throat. How, she wonders did her children become so pedantic, so articulate? And when? She thinks of 'ch' words, like chivvy and chasten and chill, muttering them under her breath. Words like chicken. Christ! She forgot the chicken while her mother was flailing at the egg counter.

Karien's mother starts whistling again, making it harder to concentrate on the driving. The pitch flattens and the cars seem to come faster. The children ask for mints. While their grandmother scrabbles in her handbag, guessing that she'll want one too and if she's sucking she can't whistle, but she hands them one each and picks up her tune again.

The girl says, "That'll do for today, thanks Gran," polite as you please, but her grandmother continues.

The boy sighs. "It's enough, please Grandma."

"Whistling polishes my halo," says Grandma, pursing her lips.

"You got a halo, Gran?"

"That and more." Karien's mother puts on a gravely voice and bats her eyes.

"What else you got, Gran?"

"Wouldn't *you* like to know?"

Karien intervenes, anxious lest the conversation turn smutty. She asks her son if he got his science project in on time. Her mother starts again. This time the children join in, each with a different tune, mocking.

Last time she scolded them, she said, "It's not funny. Gran gets disoriented. You make it worse when you tease."

Her son said, "The duvet might be on the bed, but the down is still on the duck." He was right. At 72, her mother was still in the best of health.

Karien glances in the rear-view mirror as her son crosses his eyes, slack-jawed and her daughter does a tongue waggle. She listens in on half a conversation, overhears her daughter saying, "… maximum rooster crouton."

"What's that?" says Karien, remembering she wanted oil and onions too, thinking that closure is a very long way off.

"Code," says her son, "doesn't translate."

Dove Window

Her husband plays the organ. She tells him she's there to support him, but she doesn't want to be apart from him any more, not even for an hour.

She sits in the side chapel, out of sight of the priest, away from the worshippers. The sermon is about the grain of wheat that must be planted in the ground to die before it will bear fruit.

She doesn't participate in the service, won't sing or recite the liturgy. She huddles into her book when the well-meaning approach to share the peace. She'd like to block out the sound, taking in only the diffuse light, green and gentle on the dark polished wood, the deep red carpet. The priest's words are too brittle, shards of ominous promises shattering reason and hope.

The stained glass window in the stone recess is a memorial to a 19-year-old killed in a flying accident in 1968. She wonders if his parents still come to the side chapel to remember their son, if they find comfort here, whether they are still alive. If she waits here long enough, will she be comforted too?

After the service, while the congregation sips bitter tea in the churchyard, she photographs the stained glass window. She will write on the back of the photograph a message to her child in hospital: *Wishing you light for your soul, my darling. Please don't mess with your karma . . .*

She does not envy the airman's parents the mantle of their respectable grief. But what if there is a next time for her child, like there was a last time, and if, in that next time 'failed' becomes 'successful'? Her sorrow will fill every cathedral on earth. Would even one memorial window shudder in sympathy?

The Air of Words

A pale pink slug emerges from between Josie's teeth onto the dental floss that is wrapped so tightly around her thumbs that they bulge like purple grapes. Her teeth are too close together. That's the reason she gets cavities, said her dentist. She saw him three weeks ago. When she pulls the floss between them, it snags. Josie wiggles it back and forth under pressure, trying to ease it through. When she gets it right, the floss slides down without bumping her gums, the slugs are a pale creamy colour. When she doesn't, the floss jerks through biting her gums. They bleed, giving the slugs a pinkish gloss. She squashes them between her fingers. The slimy accretions of the day smell grim even though she hasn't eaten a thing.
She regrets touching them because her fingers stink all day with the odour of what she is afraid to say – dark thoughts sticking between her teeth, seeking protection from the air of words.
The dentist referred her to an orthodontist who suggested braces. This is not going to happen. She drops the sour skein into a rubbish bin overflowing with tissues and empty toilet rolls, but it is three weeks since she last cleared the bathroom bin. At night the slugs slither up the edge of the bin, joining forces, surfacing as one giant entity that creeps up the passage, over the carpet. A pink and cream zebra-striped monster approaches her bed and covers her face.
She wakes as the slugs crawl back into her mouth. This is why she can never have braces, why she cannot throw out the garbage, why she stopped eating three weeks ago. There are things she cannot say because the slugs are guarding her tongue.

Harp

Before I turned six my third sister was born. Dad said five women were enough. The harem was complete. Estelle was beautiful. Everyone said so. Her name meant 'star'. But I was still cleverer. That Christmas I drew an angel with a harp and said, Look, Mum, I drew a 'hark'; knowing the correct word, hoping she'd laugh, think me cute. I hoped I'd overhear her tell this to my grandmother on the phone later. I tried to make droplets of water from the tap hover on my cheeks, like the crying poster girl. I wished an artist would draw me looking sorrowful. I practised turning my eyes down in the mirror above the mosaic tiles. My mother let me touch Estelle's soft fontanel, explaining that if I conked her on the head by accident, she would be brain damaged. Instead I bit her finger when nobody was looking. When my mother came through and found me comforting the new baby, she said I was a good girl, her little helper.

Under-9 Cricket XI

I tell my captain I must go to the dentist, produce the appointment card as proof, cancel the dentist and go to watch my boy play cricket instead. He does not know I have come to watch his looping slow left-arm spin. It is sweet to watch him play even though he can't see me because he is down on the pitch below, my son, down there in front of me and I on the bank above, with the sun in my eyes. I stand with the other mothers watching their boys field that hard red ball flying fast and sure. The mother beside me waves to her boy, waves with her hand full of diamonds, waves to her boy who knows where to look for her, knows she is there. But my boy does not look my way.

After her boy has waved back the other mother says, we didn't expect to see you back. Then she asks me how I am, how are you *really*. Fine, I say, just fine. She wants to know how my new posting is going, politely enquires if things are still so bad in Soweto. But I do not want to talk to her, don't want to notice her surreptitious stare at my uniform, don't want to acknowledge her wondering whether I'm as corrupt as the constables caught on TV. She chews her distaste like a nervous tic. I do not take my eyes off my son so I can't envy her pretty polished toenails, manicured rubies in strappy sandals.

No, I won't think about my ugly boots and painful feet. I do not want to say, yes, it is a safe job for a white woman in Soweto. Because it isn't. I do not want to say, no, it is hideous and horrifying because her phoney concern makes me feel small, feel less than her, this mother with a hand full of diamonds. I do not want to look away from my boy, to make polite conversation, but I do. I would not look away if my boy knew to look my way, to see me looking back at him, but he doesn't. And when I look for him again, my boy is gone.

The Cricket Eleven is now only ten, but the game goes on. It is nearly finished. Soon I must go back to my captain and rub my jaw, feign a thick lip, slur my speech and appear in pain. I walk down the hill to the edge of the pitch and ask the coach where my boy is. I tell him my boy was fielding and then he disappeared. What boy, ask ten boys standing around, staring at my uniform, making boy salutes, marching like clowns. I say, Where is my boy?

One boy says he turned into a giraffe and stalked back to the bush, two say he flew away with the pigeons, three tell me he hopped into the grasshopper's grass, four pull their sunhats lower over their eyes and look sideways at each other. An eleventh child returns from the change room. It is not my boy. The coach is new, he looks bewildered, asks my boy's name, says Ma'am, I'm sorry, your son didn't play today, says let me phone the games master to find out if he's playing at another venue. He makes a call on his mobile, but before the games master has answered, I turn to leave. Ten boys laugh at the police officer that has lost a child. It is never sweet to lose a child.

What You Really Need

Jim lounges beside me against the counter in crinkled chinos and a crisp denim shirt.

"Tired?" I ask.

"A little shopping goes a long way," he says, slipping his veined hand under my sleeveless blouse. He teases my bra strap, plucking and releasing it.

"We're nearly done. This is the last item on the Christmas shopping list."

The clerk who gift-wraps the embroidered towels I have chosen for our eldest granddaughter looks about the same age as her. The girl strokes the peach satin monogram before cutting a length of red and green paper. There is a tiny engagement ring on her finger, a wistful look on her face.

"Pretty," I say.

"Nice and absorbent," she says.

"I meant your ring."

"Oh, thanks," she laughs, holding the ring out momentarily for me to admire, then resumes creasing the paper into an elaborate design. Cutting tape, she flicks it in place with swift fingertips.

I wonder if she has ever shared a tub with her fiancé. I hope he folds her in sumptuous towels afterwards, rubs her softly and unwraps her tenderly.

My eyes rest on Jim's crotch. He catches my indiscreet staring, twirls his hand through my short curls, and wraps a lock around his forefinger. It is a proprietorial gesture, an ownership. He gives a sharp tug, a private signal, a caution.

"So, when's the big day?" I look up.

"April 12th." She snips a strand of silver ribbon.

"Nice! We had an autumn wedding, didn't we?" I say, prodding Jim's tummy.

He nods and smiles. The girl blushes. She deftly twists a many-looped bow. I wish this girl glorious weather, a beautiful ceremony, and a long, happy marriage. If her groom is half as gentle between the sheets, half as patient on the pillow as my blue-eyed lavender-tipped boy, she will be a contented bride. If her husband has anything like Jim's strong arm and judicious eye for the correct position of the paddle, if he knows when to use a riding crop and when to use his own bare hand, she will grow to be a deeply satisfied old woman.

"Merry Christmas," she says, handing Jim the parcel.

"You too," he smiles.

"Have a nice wedding," I say.

After we've gone, I think about what I should have said. I wish I had whispered in her ear, "Show him what you like. Ask for what you want. Don't be afraid to tell him what you really need!"

What's Left

The art therapist instructs us to draw a picture from our childhood with our non-dominant hand. I keep forgetting which is left and which right, but with a crayon in my hand, I am six again, playing alone. The sheep go where I tell them to, unlike my sisters. Hidden amidst the hydrangeas below the veranda, I don't have to do anybody's bidding.

Amidst the plentiful leaves and lilac blossoms I turn the slope of the flowerbed into a farmyard, engineering the drip from the gutter into a gentle stream flowing into a watering hole for my miniature cows. Pebbles reinforce the dam wall and I weave a kraal from the spines of Jacaranda fronds. My name is being called, but no one knows where I am. My sisters do not find me; my mother does not find me.

Henny-Penny, the silky bantam, plucks earthworms from the damp ground, and I say, Go away, Henny-Penny. You are too big for this game. I show her the tiny plastic rooster from my baby sister's new Fisher Price barnyard. MADE IN HONG KONG has been cast in tiny print under his left wing. I have just learned to read and I like school.

Henny-Penny says it's time for church and my mother is looking for me. She points out that my dress is splattered in mud and my new patent leather shoes are spoiled. Henny-Penny tells me to hide my shoes under the lawn mower in the cellar. There is a swallow's nest on the ceiling of the cellar, also made of mud.

This left hand journey unnerves me. I am six again and I cannot hold a crayon very well. My fingers slip around the fat stubs when I press on the paper. My letters are not neat or pretty. The girl beside me is copying my idea. I know it is a good one because my picture is better than hers. I hope Sister Anne will give me a gold star. My name is being called.

Perhaps if I finish first, she will let me light the candle at our classroom altar. It was my turn to bring flowers for the altar. I brought the fattest purple hydrangea bloom I could find in the garden, but it was too big for the little vase which overbalanced. Water spilled on the white lace cloth. The Blessed Virgin got wet too. I started to cry. Sister Anne is kind and beautiful. She says I am a good girl, a clever girl. She lets me help her, but it is not like helping my mother, which I do not like. My teacher shows me how to cut the stem shorter so that the vase would not overbalance.

I am six again and trying very hard. I want to get this picture right. Just right. I want Sister Anne to tell my mother that I am good and clever.

My name is being called, but no one can find me because I am six and for the first time in a long time, I can hear the birds.

Pickle

There are things she doesn't want her children to know,
the mother who insists on table manners when they come alternate
weekends, bringing out the knives and forks, the good nutrition:
salads and whole grain bread, organic chicken and preservative-free
juices. She allows them to serve themselves, to choose their own
portion size. She wants to teach them good things: responsibility,
to listen to their bodies, not to waste.

When they're with their father she eats alone, whole cartons of ice
cream, gobbled in private, straight from the tub, picking the crunchy
bits out with her fingers, licking the lid. The beans and tomatoes
and potatoes left in the crisper go uncooked, mouldy and tired.
Sometimes she can redeem some of the veggies, cutting off the rot
to hide them in a stew, but when the beans are finally drowning in
tears of brown pickle juice she throws them away, glad the children
cannot witness her wastefulness.

When they're with her she makes them brush their teeth,
she gives them vitamins, she tells them to take a shower. But when
she's alone, she does not always brush her own teeth, she neglects
to wash, she forgets her meds. She tells herself she is lazy. She makes
excuses, saying she is too sad. When they are with her, she doesn't
drink.

She is trying to get it all right. She really is, but it's a big job
looking after her children, even though it's only alternate weekends.
There's a lot of catching up to do for the other twelve days, the lost
time. That's the hard part.

She sends them text messages on their father's phone: *Hey sunny
boy, I love you a bucket.* She doesn't know whether he shows the
children her messages, or whether deletes them, saying only, *Mom
says Hi.* Still, she tries to make them laugh. *Hi pretty girl, your birdie
ate a humungous pawpaw..*

Maybe she should be kinder to herself, kinder to the mother, because mostly, she's kind to the kids. Mostly, but not always, and that's the thing that stays under her skin. She wishes it didn't, but it does. When she lies awake at night, she remembers the bad things: the fighting and screaming, the red welts on a surprised cheek left by her fingers, the tears and slammed doors.

The mother is tired, permanently blah. She hasn't slept in weeks, maybe years. When she left the children, she couldn't sleep for the unnatural quiet in the house. It was like her bio-rhythm had broke, expecting to wake up for one of their nightmares – snakes under the bed, wind blowing the roof off – or endless requests for milk or water. Now, she can't sleep. She wakes to the silence, no breathing in the next room.

Once properly awake, she remembers the children are gone. Then she can't get back to sleep for thinking of the freezer, the ice cream with the crunchy bits. She licks her fingers, knowing she should have taken the children with her, wishing she'd had more gumption. She should have stood up to their father.

She doesn't sleep because she is fat. Her boyfriend pats her cheek or jiggles her shoulder to wake her, telling her she's doing that funny snoring thing. He whispers that she's stopped breathing altogether; she stops again and again. She heard about a pump with a headgear you wear to sleep. She heard on the radio that if you have sleep apnoea, you wake a hundred times a night, a hundred times an hour even. You never rest, your brain always jerking awake to bring in the oxygen. Your adrenaline charging relentlessly, wears your metabolism out. Her great belly pushes into the mattress and can't push itself back up.

Alcohol, says the radio lady, is a contributing factor. She should get more exercise, but walking hurts her feet, her hip, and she's too tired to drive to the pool and swim laps after work. At work, she telephones engineers on the mines, at Kriel and Arnot and Twistdraai, telling them about training courses: diesel pump maintenance, conveyors, chute and feeder designs. She tells them about emergency power supplies conferences. But she can't concentrate, forgetting the paperwork, staying in during lunch, trying to catch up, resenting the pressure, feeling slipper-brained.

The radio lady says it can be cured. You have an assessment at the sleep clinic. They hook you up to wires, monitoring your brainwaves. They hook you up to the pump, the latest in bio-medical engineering, which gives you positive pressure all night long. It can turn your life around. You focus, work sharp, have more energy. You'll want to exercise, and without trying, you'll lose weight. It sounds like a miracle. It sounds easy. Too easy.

She's glad the garbage collection is on Friday. By the time the children come, the evidence is gone. Most of all she doesn't want her children to know that when she spends all that money on the assessment, the pump and headgear, when she stops snoring and starts sleeping, she will still let the ice cream melt enough to pick the crunchy bits out with her fingers. She will dig deep to the bottom of the tub, probing through the chocolate, smoothing it over again with her spoon, so that it doesn't look robbed.

Management of Snake Bite

1) Allay the patient's anxiety. Stay as calm as possible.

The ground in the camp is dusty but the trees are green. The tags identifying them in Latin have rusted and I don't know their English names. The bird calls are unfamiliar too, sounding like hammers on anvils, rusted hinges, rasping, grating. My daughter said I must be on the look out for the yellow-billed hornbill. She said they studied it in school. An insect flies into my eye. I wash it out with saline from the Dutch medic. I can't be bothered to read the bird book after that. My eye keeps watering. I ignore the bird search.

2) Shock can be more toxic than the bite itself. Deaths have been reported where patients have been bitten by harmless snakes.

At 9 a.m. I wind along the road towards the camp's exit under a hazy sky, wearing sunglasses. My windows are closed but dust swirls though the air vent, along with dried out seed husks, dead beetles, shards of twig and grass. I snap the vents shut then cross the dry riverbed where snakes catch frogs. I've seen the little popeyed frogs at my door, nearly stepped on one in the dark.

3) Not all snakes are poisonous.

The gap below the door to my rondavel is big enough to let through a snake, but not a frog. Before I enter, I rattle the doorknob, jiggle the door. In case. I'm scared to look under my bed. Before I put my shoes on in the morning, I shake them out. I even check the gloves of the pot holder in the kitchen, in case something has fallen from the grass roof. This wariness feels like being married again.

4) Not all poisonous snakes are fully charged with venom.

I drive in second gear, watching for buck among the thorn trees, afraid one might leap out. On the road outside the camp, I speed up, plug my earphones in, dial my ipod, looking down. I want to listen to something calming. When I look up again, the road is curving sharply. A cow is meandering across the road. It's too late to brake;

I speed up, swerving around it. Just beyond, I pull over, shaking, sweating. The Cell Block Tango from Chicago pipes through the earphone:

'He had it coming. He had it coming. He only had himself to blame.

If you'd a been there. If you'd a seen it. I betcha you would a done the same!'

5) Even snakes fully charged with venom do not always inject a lethal dose.

I recognise the trees and flowers that grow beside the public buildings as I drive into Hoedspruit: poinsettia, jacaranda, cannas and frangipani, their heady scents, the violently coloured flowers with poisonous milk that flowed from their picked stems. They grew in our Pinetown garden when I was a child. There were green mambas in those trees too. I watched the gardener kill one once. It writhed for hours after he'd decapitated it with a panga.

6) Reassurance lowers blood pressure, reducing palpitations, tremors, sweating and rapid breathing, hence reducing the speed of absorption of toxins.

We sit, my friends and I, on their patio overlooking the bush, sipping lemonade. They're the new doctors in town, a husband and wife team from Jo'burg. He does the general practice; she does the pathology and women's medicine. He asks about my eye. I dismiss it. Let me look, he says. I turn to him, he holds open the lid. It's infected already, he says. If it's not better by tomorrow come in to the practice. I'll set you up with antibiotic drops.

7) Some patients get infections or allergic reactions from so-called harmless snakes.

On the way back to the camp I drive slower, mindful of cows. My ex calls. His initials flash on the cell phone. I don't want to answer, but I'm too afraid not to. He's in Pietermaritzburg looking at church schools. He says, don't shoot me, I'm just the messenger, but Kate asked me to call you. She's sitting right here. She wants me to tell you that she's really terrified of you. She says you make her

159

feel guilty about wanting to go to boarding school. Now I'm just the messenger, remember . . .

I click off the phone and pull over, just before Jesus Loves You. I slump over the wheel, and sob.

Wonky

Pete wants to get rid of the desk. There's nothing wrong with it, but a few coffee cup rings staining the surface. I say, "Just a needs sand and a polish to fix it up like new. I'll use it for my sewing table."

He says, "If that's how feel you can do it yourself, but it goes to the back room, out of my sight."

The first time his ex left, he didn't feel too badly about it. It was better, quieter without her flinging pots of jam around the house. No more disconsolate wailing at four a.m. because the threesome she'd had with two doctors in a private ward had left her too dissatisfied to finish her shift. She'd call Pete to fetch her from work, and then pick on his driving all the way home.

She returned a year later from Merry England feeling glum, bringing back a broken heart and a newborn, another man's child. The baby had hair the colour of cream, skin translucent as bubbles. Pete loved her like his own, changing nappies, making bottles, singing 'Kookaburra' to her, because it was the only song he knew. Her mother gave up flinging pots of jam, throwing the infant about instead when it wouldn't quit fretting. Pete would take the baby away, holding her little head, letting her suck on his fingertip, jiggling her on his knee until she laughed again.

The second time Pete's ex disappeared, she took the child, leaving behind the empty cot and twenty lipsticks, colours of gashes and nosebleeds, bones and teeth. She also left the desk.

When it's time for us to move house, Pete is adamant. "That desk can't go to the new place. You'd better choose. Come with me or stay with the desk."

I say, "Don't be ridiculous. We can't afford to rush out and buy a new one."

He says, "We'll rush out and buy an old one in that case."

We traipse through junk shops in the dodgy part of town:

161

Greymont, Albertville and Triomf, where the poor whites and trying-to-arrive blacks live side-by-side. The first stop is like a set on a horror movie: barrels of disembodied mannequins, limbs and trunks and decapitated heads. In the next room ancient pews, painted cerise and orange and turquoise after being ripped from a church, are suspended from the wall. The paint peels like old whores. Chairs swing from ceiling hooks with broken legs, frayed riempies. Battered chests with lost drawers appear toothless.

The next junk shop is a repository of Afrikaner kitsch and Apartheid era municipal furniture: desks and coat racks from police stations and government offices, book shelves and cabinets that ooze dark pasts and missing people. Pete points out a chipped enamel chamber pot and tells me that it probably belonged to Betsy Verwoerd.

"We need her waltzing around in the dark," I say, "searching for her pot, pissing in the desk drawer."

Pete still hears that child crying at night and rises to settle her, sleepwalking. I find him staring where the cot used to be and steer him back to bed.

When he arranges for the shop owner to collect his ex's desk the next day, I do not argue.

At the hardware shop he checks a new pine table for a wobble. It's rough and plain as a cheap coffin. "I'll paint it any how you like," he says, standing before the colour swatch display.

"Leave it plain," I say. "Just a sand and polish." But he buys a clear finish; he knows better.

"The unvarnished truth," he says, "doesn't sit well."

An Owl at my Ankle

Today is the first day, my new teenager, since you left me as a woman. I wear your socks to work – the ones with gold stars, weird birds. Your feet now are bigger than mine, but the socks fit nicely. While I teach Grade Two to sing 'Somewhere Over the Rainbow', a turquoise owl alights on my ankle, grooms its pink-spotted wings with an orange beak, eyes blinking, polishes its glittering purple halo on its puffy breast.

It drums on the tambourine, dances on the xylophone, shakes its shoulders and flies out through the triangle dangling from the music stand. A small boy finds a curling feather under the piano stool.

"Your owl left you a message," he says, handing it to me. I look at the plume, look at the boy.

"I can't read the words," I say.

"Don't you understand Owlish?"

"No."

"It's easy," says the boy, "if you hold the feather to the light."

He stares into the sun, squints at the minute ciphers inscribed on the spine, and reads aloud to me, "I never said you could borrow my funky socks."

Dead Heads

Oupa was deaf and forgetful, becoming more so. He clacked his teeth while tying the climber rose back onto the front porch railing, tweaking off dead heads with his sharp nails. Sometimes he left his dentures on a chair or in the drinks cabinet. His skin was like tight silk, inclined to split at the smallest bump.

Dr Deek stopped by wearing red plaid trousers the day after Ma had whispered to Mrs Deek in the veggie aisle beside the pumpkins about the strange things my grandfather did at night.

When Oupa straightened, he towered over the doctor. He wiped the blood off his fingers where the thorns had scratched him and offered his hand, saying in his best English, "How might I be of assistance to a stranger on this fine day?"

Mama appeared at the railing and said, "Pa, this is Dr Deek, you know him. He stitched back your finger when you fought the lawnmower, remember? Remember?"

"Pleased to meet your Dr Geek," said Oupa. Ma pursed her lips in disapproval – perhaps because Oupa said the doctor's name wrong, or maybe because Oupa had wet himself again, or because I was giggling like a ninny. I knew to disappear, sharpish.

I ate the last six koeksusters, which I would say Oupa had given me if I was asked. But Ma never asked about the koeksusters. Not that day, or the next. Ma had other things to think about, like buying adult nappies, and fetching Oupa back from the other side of town, and making him put his clothes back on when he took them off in the middle of the day.

The Jailer

In the last weeks of my marriage I dream of isolation cells and concentration camps, soldiers on horseback, guards with guns and dogs straining at leashes snarling at lines of trudging prisoners, leading them to be interred alive. On waking I brace myself daily for the attacks that make me feel like a tethered beast. I cannot think clearly. I try to reason. I need an escape route, must make a plan. But I don't know how to leave.

My folks are in Cape Town, a thousand miles away. They don't know how bad things are. I never vent about my husband. I'm too ashamed to tell my mother that I am shattering. Still. After eleven years in therapy. And to cap everything, Cora's cancer is gaining ground. Every week my daughter seems thinner. Her skin has turned grey. She moves as if her bones are broken.

I haven't told my mother about the prolonged taunting, the ridicule, the belittling. One night near the end, my husband tells me something, then asks me what he said, but I'm confused. He tells me what he said; he tells me what I said; but even though I said it, I didn't mean it the way he's telling it. It's twisted. The meaning. He asks me if he's wrong. He is, but I can't explain the misunderstanding. He tells and asks again; pushing, pulling, pushing. My head is an over-ripe apple, my neck is the stalk, twisting, round, round, round. It snaps. I grab a knife. As I raise it, I see it pumping over and over into his carotid artery. Instead I stab the pile of dinner dishes I was about to carry to the sink. When I stop screaming, a pile of shards covers the table and my daughter is sobbing down the passage – I thought she was asleep. There are gashes in the formica and the damn tramp is sniggering at the backdoor.

Of course I'm afraid of killing myself. I've wanted to do it for so long, but I have beliefs that scare me into not doing it. I believe I am a suicide reincarnated. I have this lifetime to figure out how to survive. If I do it again, I will have to return, and next time won't be so nice. Next time will be harder. But the tramp has no beliefs. He follows me around the house, slouching in corners, watching me with his boozy eyes, always hovering. And he's started moving closer, nudging me, peering over my shoulder while I cook. I stand on his toes if I step backwards suddenly, then he shuffles into a doorway, watching and waiting. I must placate him, tolerate his terrible smell and bad habits.

I have two small children, but the tramp doesn't bother them. I teach music at a nursery school one morning a week, but the tramp doesn't follow me there. I am a Baha'i, and the Local Spiritual Assembly has informed me that if I want to get divorced I must undergo a year of patience. That means I must live apart from my husband, receiving marital counselling. If, after a year of attempting to restore matrimonial harmony, we cannot be reconciled, then we may proceed with a divorce.

The psychiatrist says I have choices: I can't get rid of the tramp, but I must make him wait on a bench outside, or tell him to sleep on the grass in the sun. I don't have to talk to him any more than that. I shouldn't listen to him. I haven't told the psychiatrist that though the tramp looks harmless, he's really a killer or that I'm having an affair, which should make me feel ashamed, but doesn't. The tramp never follows me to my lover's house. The Baha'is don't know about my affair. I know it is wrong, but I can't stop it.

A jailer has locked me in a giant hen house made of steel bars, not chicken wire, and with no protective area to nest or roost or take cover from the howling wind. The cage is set on an abandoned beach, perched on the rocks, where it wobbles and shakes at sunset. A winter storm rides in on white horses which spray over the cage, drenching my thin clothes. The tide has turned and I have never been so cold. I don't know if I will die from exposure or drown as the water rises over the cage.

A lanky figure walks along the beach. At first I think it is the tramp. Now he will get me. He will finally kill me. When the figure gets closer, it isn't the tramp. It's a thin man who knows the way out.

166

Maybe my lover, but it's too dark to see. He unlocks the cage and we steal away together. He doesn't talk, but leads me through a series of barred passages and stairs, climbing the scaffold in silence.

The Christmas Box

Annie is in a box. The one from the new fridge. It makes a good house. Bennett, her new stepbrother, said before he left that she should smarten it up. He'd be back, he said, and the place had better be ship-shape. He won't come home to a tip, no sir. Annie stays home to cook because that's woman's work. Like home decorating. And making babies. He says they will make a baby together.

On one wall she draws curtains and a window. She wants to ask Bennett what colour scheme he'd like, but he's busy at work. Decide yourself, is what he'd say.

There's no rush to cook because they just ate, even though the turkey was stringy Grandma's roast potatoes were crispy and delicious. Annie gobbled down six. After dinner they ate ice cream from the new freezer, feeling stuffed.

On another wall she draws a TV with Batman on the screen. Will Bennett like that? He's unpredictable.

Annie's Mum and Bennett's dad nap while Grandma watches TV with her hearing aid unplugged. It's difficult to draw lying on her tummy in the big box and Annie's crayons from Father Christmas snap. She'd like to show Bennett her broken crayons, but he's not to be disturbed. Men's work is important.

She draws a clock beside the TV, but loses interest, getting only to seven before her arm cramps. Men's work takes so long.
She wonders whether the place is ship-shape. She says in the silence, "Bennett, please come home."

Maybe he's out riding. On his bike. Bennett disappeared last time they played hide-and-seek together. Annie hid for hours.
He called her a crybaby afterwards. Perhaps he's gone away. Business. Travelling to see a client. But his bike is still in the garage. He might be smoking in his office.

"I won't tell," says Annie, knocking on the old fridge door.

No answer. "Come out now, Benn," she says.

Silence.

"I can't open it. This big old door is too heavy to lift. Please come out."

Rocker Surgery

Pop brought home a rocking chair from Paradise Parlour, which was not a second-hand furniture shop. My sister was seven months due. My mother said junk smelling like a thousand unwashed bums wasn't welcome. The chair didn't rock. It squeaked as it lurched drunkenly to the left. Mom didn't want a repository of other people's bodily fluids in her house, she said, glaring at my sister.

In the countdown to his first grandchild, Pop performed open-heart surgery on that chair. He unpicked the upholstery, threw out the brittle foam. The dog chewed it, littering the living room with foam confetti. Pop replaced a broken strut with a piece of the old banister that had lain in the woodpile for years. He bought a new spring and three yards of industrial denim to staple a new cover in place.

When he was done, the chair sang and danced and smelled of cotton. Blue dye rubbed off on my hands where I gripped to ride it. But my sister was superstitious. She refused to sit in it. She cried when my father forced her to.

Later, they tried open-heart surgery on the baby. It had worked better on the rocker. My sister would never sit in that chair. She said the chair remembered. It stole her luck.

You Pay for the View

At Moyo the waiters wear ostrich feather crowns and curlicues of white dots painted on their dark faces. Kate's camera pulses in her pocket, wanting to take their pictures, but her son rocks his chair in the gravel, bumping the table.

His sister slides the menu out of reach and says, "Quit being a doofus."

Kate says, "Guys, please. Manners."

The wishy-washy arrives with scented rosewater, warmed for the ritual washing. She dips into a half-kneel, singing and pouring the warm water over their hands, 'Izandla ziyagezandla'. The one hand washes the other. It's a proverb, like I scratch your back, you scratch mine. Kate's mother's voice is dinging in her head: translate the song for the children; distract them from their spat; this is a golden opportunity to teach them about their heritage, multi-culturalism; wake up.

But she does not. The children are hungry and scowling, not welcoming lectures on heritage and language or Zulu proverbs. They are mad at her because she had warned them that they would only be ordering drinks at Moyo, explaining that the restaurant was pricey and reminding them that she was out of work for a month. Her daughter said, "You pay for the view." She had told them before they left to grab a sandwich or apple so they wouldn't be hungry, but they'd refused, saying it was too early to eat.

The cappuccinos arrive sprinkled with cinnamon; the milkshakes have a swirl of cream topped with a coffee bean. The daughter says loudly, "This place is a tourist trap." Instead of simply wincing, or pulling her shawl tighter, Kate chides her when the waiter leaves: "That may be so, but these guys are creating employment, helping folk earn a living." Kate should stop, but she can't: "You don't have to put it down, you know?"

Tears ripen in the girl's eyes. She snatches her sunglasses.

She hadn't intended all that. She was trying out new words, like she did at three and four and five, when Kate would clap her hands, smiling.

At fifteen the girl wants her mother to notice her new acquisitions, like the third ear piercing, or the cherry red bra strap that peeks out her black top. She hopes Kate will laugh, or raise an impressed eyebrow.

Kate stretches across the table to pat her hand, wanting to comfort her, to apologise, but the gesture is too heavy. The girl pulls away, still injured. The boy kicks the gravel.

Kate takes out her camera and points it at a tree growing skew.

Bogtown Mazurka

Last month, when I went in for the surgery on my left bunion, the woman in the next bed removed her hospital gown, revealing breasts as long and listless as her ratty grey plait. She was scheduled for shock treatment. "I'm a boa constrictor," she stage whispered through dodgy dentures.

Her daughter tottered on kitten heels, high enough to make my remaining bunion throb. Purple satin poodles promenaded along the hemline of her full-circle skirt. Her hair was the same shade under a jaunty newsboy cap.

She told me in the same stage whisper that her mother's real name was Margaretha Magdalena Katarina Koos. "But call her Lola, like the showgirl."

"She wants yellow feathers," I said sniffing, but it came out as a snort.

"Humour her, why don't you?" said the daughter.

They sucked on their false teeth in unison, hissing an off-kilter duet.

Later the snake slithered over to my bed holding up her bosom and swaying her hips as she recited lines from Oklahoma, South Pacific and Guys and Dolls.

"Don't you love the roar of the greasepaint, the smell of the crowd?"

"Sure do, Dolly Dog," I said, forgetting her name, remembering the poodles I'd clipped and groomed in my time.

"Vicious snark," she said, slapping me. I wiped flecks of spittle from my face. Her breath smelled like the sulphurous bog downtown, where the will o' the wisp leads travellers to their end.

"Didn't mean anything by it," I said, pressing the button for the nurse, who arrived panting. I told her Lola should put her clothes back on. On her way out, she bumped into my grandson and wiggled her bum at him, saying, "Your mother wears army boots."

Today the doctor is fixing up my right bunion and removing my ingrown toenails, so my grandson has bought me an ipod. He's downloaded podcasts from the BBC for me to listen to.

"Plug into the fun stuff, Grandma," he says, fixing the earphones in place. "Ignore the tit-naked crazies." He switches on a Chopin waltz that starts out evenly, but soon crumples my sheets into lumpy chords.

"Nurse," I say, "the rhythm's not right." She plumps the pillows and pats me on the head before slipping a pink half moon under my tongue. The clouds shimmer; Chopin shapes up.

Poodle girl asks the boa constrictor, "If you were a fish, what type of fish would you be?"

I'd be any type of fish that doesn't suffer from bunions, but really I want to be a terrapin on terra firma. Aquatic excess makes me woozy. My head swims. My ears float out along the corridor, where my grandson speaks to his boyfriend.

"Tomorrow, Babe . . . I promise." He catches me staring at him and winks. "Old girl's doing well." He blows me a kiss and says, "The nurse says Grandma is keeping her clothes on."

100 Papers

Joe had spent the morning practising the accompaniment of *Footloose*. It bored him already and a six-week rehearsal schedule at Bryanston High had just begun. Extended hammering chords guaranteed tendonitis and the glissandi had formed blisters on the back of his middle fingers. There was neither beer in the fridge, nor chocolate in the pantry.

He pocketed the scrawled shopping list stuck on the fridge door with a magnet and walked to the Spar five blocks away. At the bottle store he picked up a six-pack of Castles. He was glad Marcia had left a short list. Next he grabbed three bars of dark chocolate and then bread, milk, eggs and cheese. The last item was hard to decipher: 100 paper. . . or papers?

Marcia's doctor's handwriting was illegible, but he hated calling her at work. The cashiers could often figure out what she wanted. A young woman with the green and red overall walked him to the stationery section, selecting an exam pad from the shelf.

Croxley. A4 Examination Pad. Feint & Margin. 100 pages.

It looked right. He collected a *Mail & Guardian* at the till and paid for his goods. Back at the studio, he had time for a beer or a crap. Not both. The former would help him deal with Jayde's mother; the latter more urgent.

Jayde was a sweet six-year-old with missing teeth who'd started piano lessons with him three months earlier. She could play C, G and D major scales perfectly over one octave, hands together. She was nearly finished John Thompson's *Easiest Piano Course*. She'd made excellent progress. The week before her grandmother had returned from her holiday and suddenly the letter names hovered above each note, pencilled in with the old woman's spiky script. She'd added fingerings below for good measure.

Joe had challenged Mrs Cilliers with some trepidation. Judging by the speed with which she pulled up in her Lexus, he'd intuited that she was unlikely to permit her daughter to discover her own natural learning pace.

"This is taking way too long," she complained in response, tapping her French manicure insistently on the lid of the piano. "Maryna Hertzog is playing a Haydn concerto with the Johannesburg Youth Orchestra next month. We want to fast-track our daughter's musical career."

Joe endeavoured not to roll his eyes. He wanted to say that the fast track was for athletes, not pianists, that Maryna's precocity was monkey tricks, not the child's inherent musicality. He wanted to explain his teaching method.

"If Jayde develops reading skills, she'll be able to . . ."

"Ouma has been a church organist for fifty years. Musical talent runs in the family. She can help you."

"I prefer the method that ensures long-term development of the . . ."

"No, no," said her mother. "Ouma's way will be much faster."

"Maybe Ouma should take over as Jayde's teacher?"

Joe had liked that idea, but Mrs Cilliers said that Ouma travelled too much; the interruptions to lessons would be unsettling. He wanted to say that Jayde needed consistent, not conflicting, information, but Mrs Cilliers' cellphone rang and she'd stepped outside to complete the call in privacy.

Joe looked at his watch. There was plenty of time before the lesson. He took his newspaper into the bathroom. Reading the leader article he sighed at the rugby bosses rubbishing each other. He reached for the loo paper and discovered an empty cardboard cylinder spinning on the dispenser. He studied the glob of hardened glue holding one last scrap of double-ply in place.

The doorbell rang even though the Cilliers were only due in eight minutes. They could wait. The lavatory window was open a chink. The familiar scent of Estée Lauder s 'Knowing' wafted into the room from the courtyard. Marcia occasionally wore that perfume.

"Don't you want to wait in the car, Ouma?" said Jayde, her footsteps crunching on the loose gravel of the path.

"It's nice in the sun."

"I'm coming," said her grandmother.

"You won't fight with Meneer, like Mama does?"

"Not at all; I'm here to give your Meneer a couple of tips.

Joe unfolded the newspaper and ripped through the scowling Markgraaf, crumpling the glowering Van Rooyen with the same rubbing-washing action he'd used on telephone directory pages in the long drop many years earlier.

He thought about refusing to answer the doorbell again. Ever. He was glad of the newspaper. The exam pad would have caused paper cuts.

CREDITS

Many of the prose poems and flash fictions in this collection were first published in other journals and anthologies. The publisher and the author wish to thank and credit the following journals:

Smokelong Quarterly: *Shopping List, Green Socks, White Lies, Slam*
Opium: *The Organist*
New Contrast: *Bump, Mrs Popcorn, Purification, Overture, Pickle*
Per Contra: *The Jailer, Management of Snakebite*
Gator Springs Gazette: *How the Oreo Stole Christmas, Clutter, Late*
Snov*vigate: *Litter-Bugs*
Sweet Magazine: *Thorn*
Duck & Herring Review: *Bridgework*
Mad Hatters' Review: *Text*
Insolent Rudder: *Ashram, Saviour*
Konundrum Engine Literary Review: *Duet*
Unlikely Stories: *Spider Salad, Promise, Goggles*
The Green Tricycle: *Zebra Teeth*
Wild Strawberries: *Epilogue for a Gun Running Son*
Moondance, Delmarva Review: *Kleintjie's Saint*
Open, an erotic anthology published in 2008 by Oshun Books: *Vanilla Silk, State Theatre, Juicy Lucy's Salvation, Christmas Eve Picnic, Pretoria, The Science of Curves, Fan Mail, What You Really Need*
elimae: *Prescription, Viola Practice*
Chimurenga: *Waiting for the Lotto, Mango Chutney, Lollipop*
Doorknobs & BodyPaint: *The Virtue of the Potted Fern, Mr Fixit's Lament*
Noö Journal: *Dusters*
The First Line: *My Mother's Diary*
Write Between the Lines: *The Piccolo Blues*
Mytholog: *Fist Mountain*
New Coin: *Parrot Syllabus, Sun Dried Tomatoes, Under my SAPS*

Star, Idioms
Brittle Star: *Sawubona Mfowethu!*
3:AM: *Oprah's Girl, Prognosis, Dead Heads*
The Binnacle: *Prometheus's Child*
Fidelities: *A Hundred Times a Day, Beached*
Night Train: *Bionics*
The Southern Review: *Practise, Button*
Ghoti: *New Word*
Carapace: *Fog*
The Mississippi Review: *One Hundred Babies*
Green Dragon: *Vessel, The Corner of my Eye...*
The Commonwealth Broadcasting Association: *Bassoon Lesson*
Grimm Magazine: *Perfect Timing*
Wigleaf: *Flaw*
Right Hand Pointing: *Harp*
Sleeping Fish: *Under-9 Cricket XI*
The Hiss Quarterly: *What's Left*
Salome: *Rocker Surgery*
FRiGG: *The Corner of my Eye*
The Beat: *100 Papers*
wordsetc.: *In the Biscuits, Suspect*

Printed in the United States
By Bookmasters